PLANTS & FLOWERS
FOR LASTING DECORATION

Jean Taylor

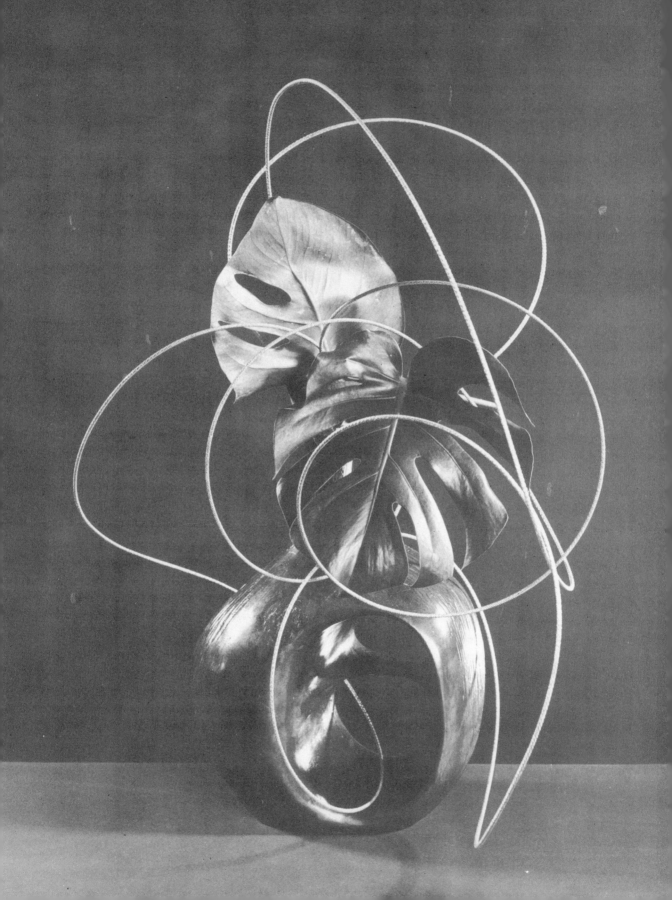

PLANTS & FLOWERS
FOR LASTING DECORATION

Jean Taylor

B T Batsford Ltd London

ACKNOWLEDGMENTS
My special thanks go to my husband Bertie, and to Dr Joe Jacovelli and
Dr Irvine Delamore; they will know my reasons.

I would also like to thank my flower-arranging friends who so kindly
provided photographs, and Paula Shea, my editor, for her enthusiasm
and efficiency.

The author and publishers are grateful to the following for supplying
photographs:

Colour
The Flower Arranger: 7, 8; H. Leadbetter: 4; Douglas Rendell: 1, 2, 3, 5, 6

Black and white
Amateur Gardening: 43, 44; Edith Brack: 20, 21, 22, 23, 25, 29, 32,
48, 57, 60; The Bulb Information Desk: 42; Carleton Photographic
Services Ltd: 55; County of Surrey Flower Arrangement Association:
7; *The Flower Arranger:* 26, 49, 50, 53, 54, 58, 63, 64; Jeremy Hall:
52; Peter A. Harding: 18, 27; Scott Lauder: 19, 31, 40; H. Leadbetter:
56; Michael Minifie: 28, 30; Douglas Rendell: 1, 2, 3, 5, 6, 9, 10, 11, 12,
13, 15, 17, 24, 36, 38, 39, 41, 65; Harry Smith Horticultural Photographic
Collection: 4, 8; Michael Warren: 45; Rodney Wright-Watson: 59.

Frontispiece A modern arrangement of cane and monstera deliciosa

First published 1981
© The estate of Jean Taylor 1981

ISBN 0 7134 2131 2

Printed in Great Britain
by The Anchor Press Ltd
Tiptree, Essex
for the publishers,
B.T. Batsford Ltd,
4 Fitzhardinge Street, London W1H 0AH

Contents

List of colour plates

between pages 96 and 97

Introduction

It is difficult to imagine rooms without plants and flowers nowadays; they are so much part of our lives and can be seen in almost everyone's home, both here and abroad. Houses without plants and flowers seem sterile and cry out for something green and living. They make a room look more lived-in because they add colour and interest, in the same way as lamps and paintings. But they also add life and a contact with nature that so many of us need.

These days the price of oil has risen so much that the trade's greenhouses have become enormously expensive to heat. In turn this has made plants and flowers expensive to buy. It has become necessary to economise and to find ways of growing plants and arranging flowers in our homes without great expense. Fortunately this is not difficult. Beauty is often enhanced by restraint and there is no need for huge bouquets of flowers. There are many long-lasting decorations that you can make using plants, bulbs, a few fresh or dried flowers, preserved leaves, driftwood and combinations of these. In addition many of the more restrained flower arrangements, plant groupings and other permanent decorations using plant material are most economical and time-saving. Once made they can stay in position for weeks and even years.

This book provides ideas for long-lasting decorations using plants and flowers and gives practical easy-to-follow details on how to make them.

1 Plants grouped together form a feature in a bare corner of a room. This is a mixture of hanging bowls and plants in their own pots. (*Arranger* Jean Taylor)

1 GROUPING HOUSEPLANTS

A bowl of several different plants is the favourite decoration in my home because, although I love flower arrangements, a busy life prevents me from making them as often as I should like. Several bowls of plants placed in empty areas provide me with permanent decorations to give life and colour to our rooms; if I make a flower arrangement it is easy enough to move the bowls to other positions.

In a sense these plant decorations have the good characteristics of both plants and flower arrangements; they combine the long-lasting quality of plants with the impression of design given by a flower arrangement. If you feel they lack the brilliant colours of flowers it is easy enough to add a few from time to time.

House plant decorations are being used more and more in people's homes and as gifts; they are especially suitable to send to a patient in hospital. Their attraction, ease of maintenance and long life are ideal qualities, but it is surprising how few of the many available houseplant books describe how to combine plants successfully.

Pots of single plants can appear rather formal, isolated and uninteresting and I much prefer to see a grouping, whether in one bowl or in many pots placed near together either in a bare corner, on a windowsill, in the fireplace in summer or on a table. The plants become an important feature in a room and there is a greater sense of design in one large grouping than in a series of single pots dotted about. Not all plants are suitable for grouping, however, and the distinctive shapes of some are better seen alone, but the majority combine success-fully.

Apart from being long-lasting and attractive, plants are good companions and thrive together, benefiting from the humidity supplied by transpiration from neighbouring plants. It is also considerably quicker to water and feed one large bowl of plants or a group of pots placed together, than single plants in different areas of a room.

There are three ways of grouping plants:

1 The plants can be removed from their pots and the roots planted in the same compost in one large container.

2 The plants can remain in their pots but can be grouped in one large outer container.

3 Separate pots can be placed close together but not united by a larger outer container.

GROUPING PLANTS

Plants removed from their pots

This type of decoration has a greater sense of design and does not need such a large container as one that has to hold several individual plant pots.

You can buy a bowl of mixed plants prepared by a florist or from a garden centre. They tend to be expensive initially but good value in the long run. Alternatively you can buy the plants singly and a container and compost. You can then plant it up yourself, which gives greater flexibility, enables you to suit it to the position in which you need the bowl and is normally less expensive. In addition you have the fun of creating your own decoration.

Containers

First choose your container. It is important to take care when making the choice because it will be in use for a long time.

These are the qualities to look for when choosing a container:

1 Sufficient depth for the amount of compost necessary to allow the roots to spread out as the plants grow.

2 Width across the top so that the leaves are not squashed together and have sufficient light and air bearing in mind how much they will grow in a year or two.

3 A size, colour and texture to suit your room.

Shiny glazes and strong colours detract from plants. It is all too easy for the container to become dominant whereas it should enhance the plants which are the important feature. Browns, beiges, soft greens, grey-blues, with a matt texture, are all suitable, but white tends to draw your eyes away from the plants. The metal colours blend well.

Suitable containers available are modern stoneware pottery, plastic and ceramic bowls sold for the purpose by florists and garden centres. There are also Victorian wash bowls and soup tureens to be found at reasonable prices and copper bowls and deep pans if you wish to spend more money. Garden bowls are now to be found in great variety, many being moulded from old designs in simulated stone. They do have a drainage hole, however, which does not matter out of doors, but which will leak on to your furniture indoors. Plug it up with plasticine, polyfilla or similar compounds. If you have attractive containers that are not watertight, large baking tins or plastic bowls can be placed inside to hold the plants.

I made an excellent 'stone' container from a shiny white

2 A Victorian wash bowl makes
a good container for ivies and
maidenhair fern, *ananas* and small
plants of primulas and kalanchoe
buds. A bunch of daffodils, together
with horse chestnut foliage, have
been placed in a small container
of water with a pinholder. (*Arranger
Jean Taylor*)

plastic urn bought at a chain store. Although the colour and
texture were unsuitable the shape had been cast from an old
design. I painted it with stone-coloured paint to which I added
sand to give it a texture, but you can buy ready-textured
paint.

Large self-watering pots can be bought in many sizes, both
square and round in shape. These are an excellent investment
for busy people because watering is reduced to once every
few weeks. A large palm surrounded by marantas and with
other plants added from time to time has been enjoyed as a
feature of our living room for nearly ten years with three
changes of compost during that period. The square container
is on castors and can be moved around easily. The reservoir
for water is in the bottom and there is an indicator to show
when filling is necessary. It was an expensive buy but has been
worth every penny.

Troughs
Troughs are popular for window sills, shelves and ledges. Plant
up in the same way as bowls. There will, however, be slightly
less of a sense of design because radiation from a central point

3 A Palm thrives in a self-watering pot in a warm, dry living room. Marantas fill the base while a *dracaena* adds transitional height. (*Arranger* Jean Taylor)

is not possible. Screw castors to the bottom of the trough if you want mobility.

Plant stands and hanging bowls

Various types of stands are available for hanging or standing plants. These may hold separate pots or groups of plants. Hanging bowls are lovely but have practical problems. To start with a hook must be provided in a ceiling or wall. It must be very firmly inserted because the pot containing plants, water and compost can be very heavy. Most suppliers of brackets and hooks for plants give the maximum weight that can be carried. It is better to use smaller bowls and plants than those used for table top decoration.

Watering is difficult at a height and you may get a shower when you try to do this, but pulleys are now available so that pots can be lowered for watering. Alternatively some people place ice cubes, which melt slowly, on the compost. However, cold water is not as suitable as tepid water for plants and could harm them.

Plants in pots in one outer container

Pots take up a lot of space and the container must be large to hold them. For this reason I prefer to remove the plants from their pots, but there are advantages in keeping each plant in its own pot; it is very easy to remove a dead or fading plant

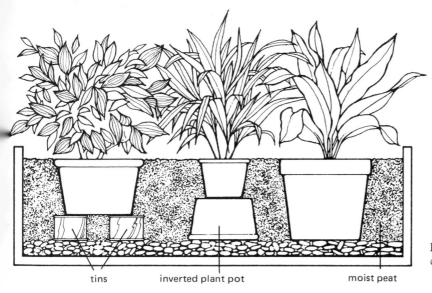

tins   inverted plant pot   moist peat

Pot plants concealed in an outer
container filled with peat

4 Plants in their own pots can
easily be replaced and gourds
conceal the pots in a large wooden
bowl

13

and you can give each plant water according to its needs.

All that is necessary is that the outer container catches drips from the water that seeps through the holes in the bottom of the plant pots, but any shallow dish, and even a tray, will do this.

The plant pots are not attractive and need to be concealed. This can be done with peat, moss, gravel, spreading plants, pebbles, gourds or bark, but make sure that you can see when a plant needs water. To provide a more moist atmosphere it is a good idea to stand the pots on pebbles or gravel. Water drains into them and slowly evaporates around the plants. The pots should not normally stand in water.

Plants in pots placed together, no outer container

Plant pots have drainage holes so it is essential for them to be placed on a plant saucer or in a decorative outer container without drainage holes. Plant pots are available in many colours and textures. The majority, however, are on the small side, which means placing small plants in them. I prefer a decorative pot to take larger plants, mainly because the compost dries out quickly in small pots and they need more frequent watering, which is time-consuming.

When grouping a number of pot plants you will usually end up with an assortment of pots in different styles and materials. This does not matter much because the plants will tend to conceal the pots, but ideally a more harmonious effect is obtained using pots of the same style and material.

CHOICE OF PLANTS

Environment

Plants do not all thrive in the same conditions of light, heat and moisture. Some like a warm room, others a cool one, some need copious watering, others sparse; some thrive in more light than others. How easy it would be if all plants thrived in the same conditions. But this is the secret of having healthy plants — to find the right conditions. This is made easy for us now; there are plenty of books supplying notes on the requirements of different plants, and most plants carry labels showing the preferred conditions. Check when buying and keep the label for reference.

Ideally plant groups should contain plants requiring the same conditions of light and heat, but it is not the end of the world if one plant dies because the conditions are unsuitable; it can be replaced easily. Most of us tend to expect plants to last indefinitely but it is really better to throw away a sickly plant than to fuss over it.

If you decide to plant several plants in one container, they should ideally be varieties that require the same amount of moisture as well as heat and light; however, plants remaining in their own pots can be provided with different amounts of water. For example a hydrangea and a mother-in-law's tongue

14

5 Spider plant, ivies, *ananas*, ladder-back fern *fittonia* provide a contrast in leaf shape with cut flowers to give height without concealing the picture. (*Arranger* Jean Taylor)

would be poor companions in the same bowl because the hydrangea needs copious watering while the mother-in-law's tongue needs almost none. These plants are better kept in separate pots.

Design

When planting a bowl of plants yourself, with the plants removed from their pots, you need to consider the habit of growth, the leaf shapes and the colours of the plants you intend to combine. These design considerations also apply to plant groupings in separate pots.

Habit of growth

Plants can be tall, trailing, bushy or spreading. A trailing plant is good for softening the edge of the container, although if its intended position is over a drawer or cupboard door it will get in the way. But trailing plants are excellent in hanging containers.

Tall, slender plants are not common and mother-in-law's tongue is a favourite to use in groupings, but it may need early replacement because the stems become soggy with normal watering. Height can always be obtained with trailing plants such as ivies or vines tied to a stick for support, with cut flowers or with driftwood if a tall plant is not to be found.

15

Bushy and spreading plants are essential for filling in the bowl and fortunately there are many of these.

Leaf shapes

Leaves come in many different shapes (see Chapter 4 on foliage). Similar shapes used in one pot can lack the contrast that gives interest to a plant community. I like to mix some medium-sized plain leaves with strap-like and fern-like foliage for variety. When buying plants place them in a group in the shop before buying; in this way you can easily see if the shapes are contrasting and whether they have different habits of growth.

Colour

Apart from contrasting leaf shapes and different habits of growth, the patterns and variations of colour in plants also add great interest to mixed bowls. The most uninteresting pots of combined plants are those in the same shade of green, and this is quite unnecessary. Plants come in many shades of green, as well as yellows, browns, reds, and even greys and mauves. Some plants have leaves in lovely patterns such as the fibrous-rooted and rhizomatous begonias, cyclamens, marantas and aluminium plants. Others have variegated leaves, for example ivies, tradescantias, peperomias, mother-in-law's tongues, coleus and spider plants.

A croton is always a temptation because of its glorious colouring, but it is not a good buy for it requires special care, being intolerant of any changes in temperature.

You may like to combine plants to suit your colour schemes and this is not difficult. Gold, yellow and green, or reds and greys, can be used together, and the addition of cut flowers or a flowering plant can add a necessary hue to pick up the colours of a nearby curtain, ornament, lamp or cushion. This gives a colour link in your room.

Health

Look for healthy plants when you buy. There should be no wilting of leaves or signs of disease. Roots should not be appearing from the top or the bottom of the pot. The compost should be damp and not dry. There should be young buds or shoots visible. Unless you buy a good plant to start with, you will have to replace it sooner than you wish.

MAKING UP A POT OF PLANTS

You will need:
Large container
Plants
Bag of John Innes No 2 compost (from a garden centre)
Pebbles, broken crocks or gravel (from a garden centre or builder's yard)
Charcoal (from a garden centre or art shop)

Method

1 Wash the container well and water the compost if it seems dry.

2 Place a 1-2 inch (2.5-5cm) layer of pebbles, shingle or crocks on the bottom of the container. These allow water to drain into them and are necessary in order to stop the plant roots becoming waterlogged, thus killing the plants. The pebbles take the place of a drainage hole.

6 Blues, whites and greens with grey driftwood form an unusual colour scheme. The plants and cut flowers are arranged in a slate-blue urn. (*Arranger* Jean Taylor)

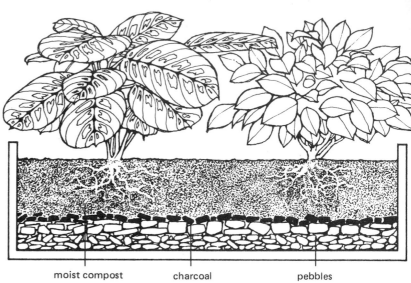

Right Pot plants planted together in one container

moist compost   charcoal   pebbles

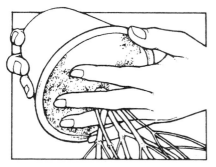

Turn the pot upside down and catch the plant between your fingers

Arrange the plants on top of the compost temporarily to see the effect

Firm the plants down, making sure compost level is below container level

3 Crumble some sticks of charcoal over the pebbles to avoid sour-smelling water.

4 Add compost to the bowl but do not fill it.

5 Remove the plants from their pots. This can be done by squeezing plastic pots or by turning a pot upside down and rapping it on the edge of a table (over newspaper). The plant should fall into your hand.

6 Arrange the plants on the compost but do not firm in until you are satisfied with the composition. Plants can be placed on their sides as well as upright.

7 Push the root ball of each plant into the compost so that it does not stand above the rim of the container and add more compost in the gaps. Firm in the plants.

8 It is *most important* to leave at least 1 inch (2.5cm) between the top of the compost and the rim of the container so that the plants can be watered. I have often been given a bowl of plants and been unable to water them without the water running on to the furniture because the compost had been built up to the same height as the container.

The plants need a week or two to settle down and the bowl will then look much more attractive than it does at first.

AFTERCARE

Plants taken out of their pots

Water the compost and not the plants. Avoid a daily dribble of water and water only when almost dry, which may only be every two or three weeks according to the dryness and heat of your room. Use tepid water rather than cold.

Spray the plants occasionally to increase the moist atmosphere around them.

Feed every few weeks from March to October but avoid

feeding and much water during winter when plants have a rest period.

Pinch out the growing tip of a plant if you wish it to become more bushy.

Place the bowl in good light. Do not place it in a draught, over a radiator or television set, near an open fire, or in a hot sunny window in summer. All these positions will cause rapid drying out of the compost and the plants will become damaged.

Many plants will endure cold rooms but the rooms should be frost-free.

Plants grow towards the light and it may be necessary for good balance to turn the bowl sometimes or to place it in another position. This means that one plant will not grow and lean to the light more than the others.

It is not necessary to change the compost more than once a year but I find each spring that I need to remove fading plants and renew the compost; in other words a spring clean is necessary. Spring is the best time because the plants are then ready to begin new growth.

Plants can be replaced at any time if they die by placing newspaper under the bowl and lifting out the dead plant.

Dead leaves and flowers must also be removed occasionally.

Plants left in their pots

The cultural requirements of plants are the same whether they are removed from their pots or remain in them. For example, a hydrangea always requires a lot of water. This is why it is important to combine plants that like the same conditions when they are removed from their pots and grouped in one container.

ADDITIONS TO GIVE INTEREST

The plants in a bowl are sufficiently decorative on their own for everyday use but you can add interest from time to time with other plant material or accessories such as:

Baubles on sticks, or tied to the stems, for Christmas
A small oil lamp or candle holder on a stand to provide a soft light for a party
Pieces of bark to fill spaces or add height
Small plants from the garden such as snowdrops, primroses, polyanthus
Flowering plants from a florist such as poinsettias for Christmas, African violets, small azaleas, gloxinias, cyclamens
Sea fan, coral, shells
Driftwood to add height
Bulbs such as hyacinth (in bud for longer life)
Rocks of good shape and colour
Cut flowers and foliage

7 A small oil lamp adds soft light to a bowl of growing plants and cut flowers. (*Arranger* Joan Owen)

8 *Right* Plants in their own pots placed in a copper bowl with a poinsettia added for Christmas

Most additions can be inserted in, or placed on top of, the compost, but cut flowers need water and a receptacle must be provided for the mechanics to hold the stems in position.

Adding cut flowers and foliage

The name used by flower arrangers for a composition that includes growing plants and cut flowers is 'pot-et-fleur'. Insert a lidless food tin or a small plastic bowl into the compost to hold water and a pinholder or Oasis. This can be placed in any position where there is enough space and where you wish the flowers to add colour or height. The water may need topping up daily because the container must of necessity be small.

Usually the flowers are placed together because of the container of water and mechanics, but more than one container can be used for more than one grouping.

If single stems are to be added test tubes and empty cigar cases can provide enough water and be pushed into the compost. You can also use cones of metal or plastic attached to sticks or pushed into the compost to hold more than one stem. These are more difficult to conceal than a bowl but can be hidden behind plants or pieces of bark.

Suitable types of cut flower

Large bowls of plants need large flowers; smaller bowls should have smaller flowers. Clear shapes seem to be the most effective, such as tulips, daffodils, arums, roses, orchids, anthuriums, chrysanthemums (both blooms and sprays and especially the single type of spray chrysanthemum).

EASY-TO GROW FOLIAGE PLANTS FOR MIXED BOWLS

For height	Trailing	Bushy or spreading
Aspidistra	Asparagus plumosus	Adiantum
Cissus antarctica	Asparagus sprengeri	Ananas
Cocos weddeliana	Chlorophytum comosum	Anthurium
Dracaena sanderina	Ficus pulmila	Aralia
Euonymus japonicus	Hedera	Asplenium
Fatshedera lizei	Nephrolepis	Begonia rex
Ficus pulmila	Pellaea rotundifolia	Beleperone
Grevillea robusta	Peperomia	Cryptanthus
Hedera	Rhoicissus rhomboidea	Echeveria
Kentia belmoreana	Saxifraga sarmentosa	Grevillea robusta
Neanthe bella	Tradescantia	Maranta
Philodendron scandens	Zebrina pendula	Nephrolepis exalta
Rhoicissus rhomboidea		Pellaea rotundifolia
Sansevieria		Peperomia
Senecio macroglossus		Pilea
		Saxifraga sarmentosa
		Sempervivum
		Tradescantia

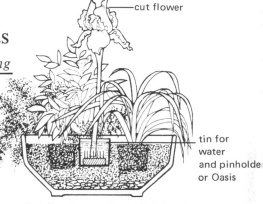

Cut flowers can be added to plant containers

9 *Left* Roses placed in cones of water (with bark to hide the cones) to add colour to an arrangement of plants

10 A maidenhair fern and a *pilea*, both small plants, need small flowers, such as spray carnations and daisies. (*Arranger* Jean Taylor)

21

Cultural details

Plant name	Plant shape	Leaf shape	Colour	Water	Temperature	Light
Adiantum maidenhair fern	spreading small, 6-10in. height and spread	feathery, very small	light green	plenty, spray	not below 65°F (18°C)	shady
Ananas comosus pineapple	rosette, 2-5ft across	rigid, sharp-edged, long	grey, var. green and cream	keep moist, dry between watering	55°-70°F (13°-21°C)	light
Anthurium scherzerianum flamingo flower	spreading, medium size, 9in. tall, 12-18in. spread	oval large, tough	red spathes like flowers, mid-green or dark green leaves	keep moist, spray	not below 60°F (16°C)	light
Aspidistra lurida cast iron plant	useful height to 12in., medium size, spread 24in.	elegant, single, long, slow-growing	dark green, glossy	rather dry, spray or sponge	cool around 55°F (13°C)	light or shade
Asplenium nidus avis birds nest fern	arching rosette, medium, fronds 2-4ft height, 1-2ft spread	single, undivided, long, oval	bright, pale green, glossy	no cold water, spray often	not below 60°F (16°F)	shady
Asparagus plumosus asparagus fern	dainty, trailer, spread 1-2ft	needle-like making a flat sheaf of feathery foliage	mid-green	keep moist, spray	cool, minimum 45°F (8°C)	light
Asparagus sprengeri	trailer, spread 3-4ft.	long fronds of needle-like leaves	light green	keep moist	cool, about 55°F (13°C)	light
Begonia rex	spreading, small to large varieties, height up to 12in., spread 18in.	asymmetrical	many, inc. grey, red, pink, green, exotic markings	rather dry, no spray	55-65°F (13-18°C)	shady
Beleperone guttata shrimp plant	spreading, medium, 12-18in. height and spread	small, grown for bracts	green leaves, bracts in yellow pink-brown	water well in summer	50-60°F (10-16°C)	good light
Chlorophytum comosum spider plant	trailer, with runners with new plants, height 10in.	long, narrow strap-like, curving, up to 12in.	green and white or all green	keep moist, water well in summer	45-75°F (8-24°C)	light or shade

Plant name	Plant shape	Leaf shape	Colour	Water	Temperature	Light
Cissus antarctica kangaroo vine	climber, with useful height up to 6ft	heart-shaped, serrated	dark green, glossy	moderate water, spray often	50-65°F (10-18°C)	good light
Cocos weddeliana palm	tall, useful height to 30 in.	large fronds, arching	dark green	ample at roots, spray	55-65°F (13-18°C)	good light
Cryptanthus earth stars	rosette-shape, small to medium, up to 18in.	hard, sharp, long	usually variegated	no cold water, moist, spray, good drainage	not less than 60°F (16°C)	good light
Dracaena sanderiana variegated dragon tree	tall stems up to 18in., spread up to 15in.	narrow, growing up the stem	grey-green and white	avoid over-water-ing, spray	60-70°F (16-21°C)	light
Echeveria	rosette-shape useful centre plant	fleshy	grey-blue, blue-green, pale mauve	little as a succu-lent, no spray	40-60°F (4-16°C)	light or sun
Euonymus japonicus golden bush	bushy, shrub-like (cut down in spring), up to 6ft	oval, many to a stem	green with yellow or white variegations, glossy, leathery	water well, spray	cool, 40°F (4°C) in winter	very light
Fatshedera lizei fat-headed Lizzie (cross between ivy and *Fatsia*)	Tall, will reach 6ft, cut back for bushy growth	three or five pointed lobes	bright green turning darker, shiny	water well, spray	minimum 50°F (10°C), hot rooms suitable	light
Fatsia japonica (Syn. *Aralia siebol-dii*) fig leaf palm	spreading, very large, height and spread 2ft minimum	lobed, large	green, green with silver blotches	water well, spray	cool, about 45-60°F (8-16°C)	light
Ficus pumila creeping fig	trailer or climber, small, 18-24in. height	small, oval, pointed	dark green	water well, spray	60-72°F (16-22°C)	good light, tolerates shade
Grevillea robusta silk oak	upright but bushy, 3-6ft	fern-like	bronze-green when young, turning green	water well but dry air	50-65°F (10-18°C)	light

Plant name	Plant shape	Leaf shape	Colour	Water	Temperature	Light
Hedera ivy	climber, trailer, or bush, small to medium, height indefinite	lobed, heart-shaped, oval	dark green, variegated green with yellow, cream white or grey, golden	moderate water, spray	45-60°F (7-16°C)	good light, tolerates shade
Howea belmoreana palm	tall, arching, up to 6ft height and spread	elegant, long leaves, fan-like with slender leaflets	green	water well in spring otherwise moderate, spray	60-70°F (16-21°C)	shade in summer
Maranta leuconeura 'Kerchoveana' prayer plant	spreading, low-growing, spread 12in. or more, height 6-8in.	large, oval	grey-green, brighter veins, dark brown patches	moist, water well in summer, spray	55-65°F (13-18°C)	light
Neanthe bella parlour palm	tall, up to 30in., slow growing, arching	fan-like with slender leaflets	mid-green	tepid water, plenty in summer, spray	55-65°F (13-18°C)	light
Nephrolepis exaltata	spreading, low-growing, medium 18-30in. height, spread indefinite	fern with fronds that taper	pale green	keep moist, plenty of water in summer, spray	minimum 50°F (10°C) no hot, dry air	light but not sun
Pellaea rotundifolia cliff brake fern	spreading, low-growing, small, up to 8in. height	small, round	green	keep moist, spray	55-60°F (13-16°C) no hot, dry air	good light
Peperomia	many species bushy, some trailing, small, height 3-10in., spread 5-9in.	small, oval or heart-shaped	green, variegated cream, white, grey or purple	mainly succulent, tepid water, keep rather dry but no spray	minimum 55°F (13°C)	good light
Philodendron scandens sweetheart plant	climber, up to 6ft	heart-shaped	mid to dark green	water well, spray	60-70°C (16-21°C)	light but not sun

Plant name	Plant shape	Leaf shape	Colour	Water	Temperature	Light
Pilea cadierei aluminium plant	small, compact, bushy, remove tips for bushi-ness, height up to 12in.	small, oval	dark green silvery patches	water well, spray, tepid water, no drying out	55-65°F (13-18°C)	moderate light
Rhoicissus rhomboidea grape ivy	climber, 4-6ft., can be a trailer	leaves have three stalked leaflets, toothed, irregularly diamond-shape	dark green, shiny	water well in summer, spray	45-65°F (7-18°C)	good light
Sansevieria trifasciata laurentii mother-in-law's tongue	tall, slow-growing, up to 4ft	single, rigid, pointed, sword-like	green or green edged yellow	minimal, should be comb-ined with succulents	minimum 50°F (10°C)	sun or good light, tolerates shade
Saxifraga sarmentosa mother-of-thousands	small, bushy, quick-growing up to 12 in., runners with young plants make it a trailer	small, circular	mid-green with silver veins, red flush below	keep moist	50-60°F (10-16°C)	very light
Sempervivum houseleek	low-growing, rosette spread 6-12in.	oval, fleshy	green, often tipped red or flushed purple	a succ-ulent so little water	cool, about 50°F (10°C)	sun or good light
Senecio macroglossus 'Variegatus' cape plant	climber or trailer, similar to ivy	thick fleshy, triangular	dark green and cream, glossy	moderate no spray	55-65°F (13-18°C)	light
Tradescantia fluminensis wandering sailor	small trailer	oval, on short leaf stalks	bright green often striped silver or yellow, pale purple under-sides	keep moist	50-60°F (10-16°C)	good light
Zebrina pendula	small trailer	oval, up to 3in. long	mid-green with two silver bands, undersides purple	keep moist	50-60°F (10-16°C)	good light

2 BASIC OUTLINE DESIGNS

11 *Below* A branch picked up on a country walk combined with a bunch of daffodils and stones to hide the pinholder. (*Arranger* Jean Taylor)

In Alabama, where I lived for some years, the summer heat made growing many flowers difficult. This meant that florist's flowers were also scarce, expensive and sold from refrigerators. With a growing family to look after, two flowers were the most I ever bought at one time – and these lasted only a couple of days. Yet because I yearned to have a few fresh flowers in my home I soon learnt ways of making the most of a small

number of flowers, using a variety of dried plant materials and accessories. Flower arrangers in many parts of the world must do likewise, because few have the abundance of flowers that we have in the British Isles.

Although some people are happy to work just with plants or just with dried flowers, others prefer to include a few fresh flowers. However, not only is this an economical way of arranging flowers, for you need only replace the faded flowers, it is also time-saving.

It is well worth while to spend a few hours working out some designs that will take only a few minutes to arrange and use only two or three flowers, thus giving a 'quick change' design, because different flowers can be used in a design, the outlines of which will remain in place for weeks. Assemble containers, driftwood, branches, accessories and then 'marry' those that suit each other and decide on the best form of mechanics. Then you are prepared for quick assembly whenever you have a few flowers and especially when you are in a hurry.

When people first start flower arranging they have few materials with which to 'stretch' the flowers, but a store is soon collected and indeed this is one of the most fascinating and pleasant activities of flower arrangement. No walk is without a 'find', whether it be branches in the countryside, driftwood by the lakeside, shells by the sea or even ornaments and other accessories in a city.

PLANT MATERIAL TO COLLECT

Branches

In winter the shapes of bare branches can be seen easily and you can cut some to keep for years. A branch is not always a perfect shape when you cut, however, and will probably need some pruning to obtain a better line.

It is advisable to cut several branches of the same variety. At least one should be tall to give height, the others being used to carry through the 'line' at another angle. If you have several branches of one kind you have a choice of shape and can vary arrangements from time to time, placing the branches in different positions.

In spring branches with buds can be cut and you can watch them gradually unfurl into leaves or flowers. Eventually they drop off, or can be removed when dead, and you are left with a bare branch of interesting shape.

When using branches a few strong lines are more effective than many weak ones. The spaces between are then well defined and it is in these spaces that you can place a small number of flowers, where they will be framed and emphasised by the branches. Two or three long-lasting leaves can be positioned to soften the rim of the container and to act as a design 'stepping

12 *Opposite right* The same branch can be used at a different angle and combined with three irises. A small bunch of flowers such as snowdrops, violets or primroses can be used at the base. (*Arranger* Jean Taylor)

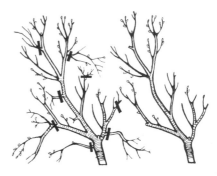

Remove unwanted foliage and branches

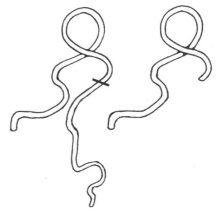

Cut trailing end for more interesting shape

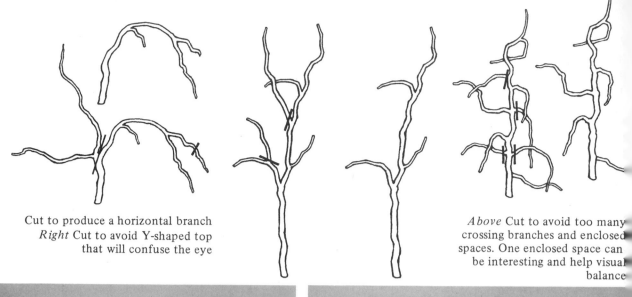

Cut to produce a horizontal branch
Right Cut to avoid Y-shaped top
that will confuse the eye

Above Cut to avoid too many
crossing branches and enclosed
spaces. One enclosed space can
be interesting and help visual
balance

13 *Above* Alder catkins can have a confused line and need pruning. The daffodils should be turned different ways with the stems centred on the pinholder for a neat, well-groomed effect. (*Arranger* Jean Taylor)

stone' between the long lines of the branches and the round shapes of the flowers.

This is a simple style of design but one that I find is infinitely satisfying, apart from being easy to make. The individual beauty of the plant material can be emphasised and enjoyed, which cannot happen when flowers are massed together. Against a plain wall the rhythmic curves of branches can be admired again and again.

Useful branches

Broom which can be curved easily with the hand and dried (see page 90).

Pussy willow which can also be curved and dried.

Ivy branches with leaves which last for months. They can be stripped of bark after several days of soaking in water to reveal the white inner stem.

Blackthorn and hawthorn which are dramatic, although prickly.

Hogweed stems which can be dried and are straight, strong and woody.

Gorse which has been burnt.

Wisteria vine, which like ivy can be stripped of bark after several days of soaking in water to reveal the white inner stem.

Red hot poker stems which dry.

Onions, leeks and other alliums which can have amazing curves.

Pine, preferably the short-needled varieties.

Pampas grass for fluffy stems.

14 *Opposite right* The same arrangement after pruning and altering the position of the flowers. The branches will give weeks of pleasure (*Arranger* Jean Taylor)

15 *Below left* Catkins and evergreens that last well provide a frame for a bunch of daffodils. The flowers can be replaced easily. (*Arranger* Jean Taylor)

16 *Below* Pine and laurel last well and make a simple arrangement with a bunch of daffodils

17 Catkins arranged horizontally are more noticeable. *Corylus contorta* with double daffodils. (*Arranger* Jean Taylor)
18 *Left Corylus contorta* with daffodils and oyster fungus in a landscape design. (*Arranger* Marian Aaronson)

Corkscrew willow, *Salix matsudana* 'Tortuosa', which is quick and easy to grow and a 'must' for flower arrangers for combining with spring flowers.

Contorted hazel, *Corylus contorta* or Harry Lauder's walking stick, again a 'must' to grow, not for its ugly summer foliage but for its incredibly curving winter branches.

Fasciated willow, *Salix setsuka,* which has textured branches that are flattened out at the tips.

Monkey puzzle tree, *Arucaria;* branches can be dried or glycerined (see Chapter 7).

Bamboo stalks when fresh, with the leaves removed, can be bent easily and are good for modern and abstract designs.

Reeds which are long and fresh can be bent easily and are also good for modern and abstract designs.

Honeysuckle vine, defoliated for outline effect.

Oriental poppy stems dried, often with dramatic curves.

Reedmace (Bulrushes) collected from the countryside (but you need to wear long rubber boots to harvest these) for dramatic straight lines.

These are some special branches to collect, but the branches of many ordinary trees can have lovely shapes. You will find them lying on the ground in the countryside, and many of my loveliest branches have been picked up in my garden after a storm.

Driftwood, roots and bark

These are great 'stretchers' of flowers and are described in Chapter 8. A piece of wood can remain in place as a decorative feature and then be brought to life with the addition of a few fresh flowers placed in a concealed container.

PLANT MATERIAL TO BUY

New and interesting plant material is constantly being introduced and once you get the idea of extending fresh flowers with these materials, you will know exactly what to buy and what suits your home surroundings. Normally it is height and line that is needed, but background material is also useful.

19 *Left* Fasciated willow leading the eye to one beautiful anthurium flower, which can last a month. (*Arranger* Marian Aaronson)

20 *Above* A branch provides an outline for two peonies (in the autumn these could be dahlias and in the winter florist's chrysanthemums) with glycerined foliage. Try different angles when positioning the branch; this one is 'upside down'. (*Arranger* Edith Brack)

Branches and leaves

Edgeworthia 'Mitsumata' from Japan with smooth straight branches which can be cut for a modern effect and interlaced.

Fasciated *forsythia* with most interesting curves and textures.

Palmetto and palm leaves which can be cut into spears or other shapes.

Palm leaves; long strappy variety which can be looped.

Coconut palm spathes and stems, with beautiful curves of very hard tissue.

Manzanita wood which is often sand-blasted, cream and smooth, or can be found in its natural state, dark red and brown.

Palm leaf fans which can be lengthened with false stems.

Opuntia, prickly pear, which can be found on beaches in southern Spain; very tall, skeletonised pieces are quite ethereal; if you find a thick piece gently separate the many layers.

Cycas leaves, which are usually glycerined, are tough and brown. When dried and cream in colour, they are less pliable but never become brittle.

Agave, dried flower stems and leaves; the tall stems and seed heads dry black, and the leaves are sword-like.

Reedmace (bulrushes), rigid, tall stems with velvety tops, brown but sometimes dyed, and sometimes the brown is shaved off to reveal a beige inside.

Poinciana seed pods which are long, curved and brown.

Dried bamboo canes in a variety of lengths and diameters; the larger ones are used as containers.

Ferns, dried, usually from Japan, sometimes bleached or dyed and very dainty.

Rattan or basket cane

Cane is also a natural plant material, sold by handicraft shops in a number of diameters for basketry. Patterns can be easily made, the cane falling into fascinating curves without any manipulation. The spaces formed give great interest in a design.

Alternatively you can soak the cane for a day or two and then wire or tie it into shapes, or wire it on to a lampshade ring for perfect circles (see page 90).

Wrack

Wrack, a seaweed, is cast ashore and can be found easily on Northumbrian and Scottish beaches. It has interesting curves and loops and dries naturally on the beach. It is advisable to bind the ends with tape or polythene when it is to be placed in water as it can re-absorb water and become soft. Wrack combines well with shells and coral for summer arrangements.

Long-lasting leaves

There are many leaves which last for weeks, even months, in arrangements, although length of life depends much on the conditions of heat and humidity in a room (see Chapter 4).

21 *Opposite left* Twelve pieces of buckthorn found on a beach and sprayed black. Scarlet gladioli are used in this arrangement but dahlias, roses or other flowers in season could be substituted. (*Arranger* Edith Brack)

22 *Right* Fasciated forsythia, which can be bought, provides an interesting outline for two long-lasting anthuriums (these could be changed for large roses, dahlias or chrysanthemums, or peonies in the summer). (*Arranger* Edith Brack)

33

23 A permanent outline of basketry cane frames two pink tulips. (*Arranger Edith Brack*)

24 *Right* Another useful design for a bunch of daffodils framed by unfolding chestnut buds with laurel leaves to hide the pinholder. (*Arranger* Jean Taylor)

They provide an excellent outline or background for a few flowers which can be changed as they fade.

Some useful leaves

Name	Description	Time to harvest	Method
Arum lily	sagittate, green	use fresh	submerge in water overnight with a little starch added
Aspidistra	oblong-lanceolate, green or variegated	any time	dry or glycerine
Aucuba	spotted, narrowly ovate	any time	glycerine
Beech	smooth oval, green or copper	July onwards	glycerine
Bergenia	mid-green leathery, rounded	cut as required	glycerine

Name	Description	Time to harvest	Method
Blue cedar	needle-like, blue	use fresh	remove lower pine needles; long drink of warm water overnight — lasts six weeks
Golden privet	ovate yellow	July onwards	glycerine
Hosta (all varieties)	broadly lanceolate, green, blue and variegated	July onwards	dry
Houseleeks	tiny clustered leaf rosettes green/blue	any time	dry
Iris	sword-like, green	July onwards	glycerine or dry
Ivies (trails or single leaves)	lobed ovate, green and variegated	any time	glycerine
Kale (ornamental)	curled and fringed pink/crimson/purple/green/white	cut as required	dry

FEATURE FLOWERS

Arrangements with permanent or semi-permanent outlines seem to need 'feature' flowers' — flowers of importance. This is partly because when only two or three are used, they need to be larger, unless many smaller flowers are bunched together. Suggested flowers are:

Amaryllis
Arums
Camellias
Chrysanthemum blooms
  (one flower to a stem)
Chrysanthemums — single spray
  (several flowers to a stem)
Clivias
Dahlias
Gerberas
Hydrangeas (mature)
Lilies
Orchids (larger ones)
Peonies
Red hot pokers
Roses (open)
Strelitzias

For the mechanics for using live flowers with other plant materials, see Chapter 7, page 107.

ACCESSORIES

Objects that are not made of plant material are also good 'stretchers' of flowers. Figurines, ornaments, shells, coral, sea

25 'Carol' roses are especially long-lasting — having been well conditioned they will give up to two weeks of beauty. (*Arranger* Edith Brack)

26 Flowers can be arranged over a fireplace when there is no fire. (*Arrangers* members of the Nottingham Flower Club)

fan, plates, cups and saucers and paintings, can be combined with flowers. Often the flowers are arranged in concealed containers and all the components are placed on a base which draws them together. It is important that the flowers, base and accessory are harmonious in colour, style and scale. Otherwise they do not appear as a complete design. All the components also need blending together to appear as one and not as separate items.

In show work the plant material must predominate over any objects that are man-made or of non-plant material.

3 MAKING FLOWERS LAST

Some people's flower arrangements look fresh for days while other people's flop overnight, which must be most frustrating after time has been spent in arranging them. So what are the secrets of keeping flowers fresh? To start with it is important to know that a dead flower and a wilted flower are different. Even a bud can wilt. A dead flower has come to the end of its normal life span, which varies from one day to several weeks according to the type of flower, and its life is therefore difficult to extend. However a wilted flower will die before its time even in the bud stage unless prevented or revived.

Wilting is not difficult to prevent – it is a matter of a little preparation before the flowers are arranged. To a busy person it may seem that time spent in preparing flowers is just one more extra job, but it really is worthwhile and takes little time. It has become such an automatic habit with me that I hardly notice when I am doing it.

The reason for wilting is shortage of water. When plant cells are full of water they support each other and the plant is turgid; since a mature plant is more than 75 per cent water, any great water loss is soon noticed. So preparation concerns water content.

Cut plant material lives longest in a cool, damp atmosphere, which is not usually found in a cosy, warm living room, ideal for humans. To take a flower from a cool garden and place it in a warm room is similar to placing a person from the British Isles in the middle of the Sahara desert. For this reason the flowers must be prepared for this onslaught of unaccustomed heat and dryness by making sure the stems are taking up water and by filling them up before they are arranged.

PREPARATION

There is a difference between the preparation of florist's flowers and those cut from a garden. It is also helpful to understand the reasons behind the various treatments.

Some people use all kinds of additives, and in *ikebana* there are suggestions for almost each type of flower. For me the transient quality of flowers does not make it worthwhile or practical to give complicated and very varied treatment that

Snip off about half an inch (1cm)
of stem ends

Place immediately in a bucket or
jug of lukewarm water

may add only a few hours' life to the flowers. However, I do believe in some quick, basic preparation.

FLORIST'S FLOWERS

Almost no preparation is necessary for florist's flowers before arranging them because the florist has done this for you. Furthermore, flowers grown for the trade are well known for their lasting qualities.

When you get home unwrap and untie the flowers and after snipping off about half an inch (1cm) of stem end place the stems immediately in a bucket or jug containing 3-4 inches (7-10cm) of water until you are ready to arrange them. If this is likely to be several hours, place the receptacle in a cool, dimly-lit room to retard the flowers' growth.

Choosing and making the most of popular florist's flowers

Florist's flowers will last much longer if you make good buys to start with. Always buy flowers that are in bud, just showing colour, when possible. They have a longer vase-life and you can watch the flowers open, which is always a delight. Sometimes a few flowers are already open on a stem or in a bunch, but make sure there are plenty of buds. You may be very taken with the beauty of open roses in a florist's but you will not enjoy them at home for so long.

Spring flowers such as irises, daffodils and tulips are generally sold in tight bud because their vase-life is short (in a garden they flower in the cool months and a warm room is not their normal habitat).

Achillea filipendulina 'Gold Plate'; narrow, tightly packed, flat heads of yellow-gold flowers on strong stems. Not stocked often but buy it when seen in autumn because the flowers dry naturally in an arrangement and can be used indefinitely for winter use. No special conditioning.

Agapanthus, African lily; spheres of small blue or white flowers in late summer, which last well and then the seeds dry for winter use. No special conditioning, the dead flowers can be removed if you do not want the seedheads.

Allium; spheres of mauve, pink or white flowers in a number of sizes, in summer. Remove dead flowers and do not condition with hot water which increases the smell of onions. Seedheads can be dried for winter use.

Alstroemeria, Peruvian lily; in many fascinating colours with markings. Small flowers clustered at the top of a long stem. The flower stems can be cut off the main stems for smaller arrangements. The trade has developed them so that they can be bought over a long season. Strong stems, no special conditioning; buy stems with some buds as well as open flowers.

Anthurium, flame flower; red, pink, white, green, sometimes mottled, flower-like spathes, expensive but can last a month. They can look almost artificial and newcomers to anthuriums tend to touch to see if they are real, because the coloured spathes are very shiny. No special conditioning unless the flowers are very young or have been out of water a long time when they need the boiling water treatment. Strong stems. Can be bought May to September and ordered specially. They are often beautifully packed with their own tubes and carefully wrapped spathes. The central spadix should be light because this indicates a young flower.

Arum lily, Zantedeschia aethiopica; large white spathes which gradually unfurl from a tube shape. Conspicuous yellow spadix in the centre should be light in colour indicating a young flower. The long fleshy stems can be split at the cut end and need binding with a small elastic band before impaling on a pin-holder. The petals should not look crepe-like but should be glistening white.

Carnation, single and spray, *Dianthus;* both can now be obtained all the year round in many colours. The flowers are smaller on the spray carnations and the stems can be cut down for small arrangements. The stems are strong and can be rigid. I look for those with a curve but they usually have a weaker stem and are rather brittle, so need careful handling. Buy when the flowers are still curled up for long vase-life. Cut the stem above or an inch below (2.5cm) a node because it is thought that the nodes can slow up water intake when left at the base of the stem. A teaspoonful of glucose to a pint of vase water is thought to be helpful to carnations but I would also add half a teaspoonful of mild disinfectant to a pint of water.

Chincherinchee, Ornithogalum thyrsoides, star of Bethlehem; small, star-shaped, white flowers in clusters at the top of the stem. Last for weeks, no special conditioning but cut off the stem end as this can be sealed with wax by the grower to retard loss of moisture. The flowers open gradually and dead flowers can be removed easily.

Chrysanthemum; single and double flowered, single bloom or sprays of smaller flowers, obtainable all year and long-lasting in water. The petals on single blooms can be incurved like a globe; reflexed with petals falling outwards and downwards and overlapping; intermediate similar to incurved but looser; single with a daisy eye; anemone centred with a similar eye but tubular florets forming a raised cushion; pompoms which are small and globular with tightly packed petals; other types such as thread-petalled or spidery blooms, spray and cascade (not seen in shops normally). There are many colours, white, pink, bronze, yellow, orange, red, rust, cream, apricot. The spray chrysanthemums with many flowers on short stems and one single main stem can be used at a height of 2 or 3 feet (60-90cm) if the flowers are not cut from the main stem. When cut they can be used for smaller arrangements. The white, yellow, apricot and bronze single sprays manage to look less autumnal than other chrysanthemums. These long-lasting flowers need no preparation other than recutting the stems; the thick woody stems of some large blooms should be slit for an inch or two. Because of their lasting quality the vase water often becomes unpleasant and this can be avoided by adding half a teaspoonful of a mild disinfectant to a pint of water. This discourages bacteria, which foul the water.

Clivia; many small trumpet-shaped flowers at the top of a stout stem, opening to a half sphere, orange flame colours, obtainable in spring. No special treatment but remove dead flowers and buy when there are some buds as well as open flowers.

Dahlias; These are not long-lasting flowers and so they should be bought when no more than half-open and without any faded petals on the outside.

Delphiniums, larkspurs, lupins, snapdragons should have no falling petals when the flowers are shaken gently and the top flowers should be in tight bud.

Freesia; sweetly scented, single and double, small flowers grouped at the top of the stem and gradually opening; the dead flowers can be removed; many fascinating colours. Strong stems and no special treatment necessary. Obtainable most of the year.

Gerbera, Transvaal daisy; brilliant colours of red, orange, pink, yellow, some pastel cream and apricot, white in a large daisy-type flower on long, leafless, strong stems. Beautiful flowers but the flower heads can flop quickly in the same way as roses. Often obtainable, but choose with care. Choose those with round, non-mouldy centres and straight stems. Remove the plastic cone used for packing, cut the stem ends, burn in a gas or match flame for half a minute or so and then place at once in a container of deep, tepid water. Leave them in a cool, dim place for at least 24 hours and preferably for two days before arranging them. They make excellent centre of interest flowers.

Gladiolus; flowers of many colours on a stout, erect, tall stem; useful for larger arrangements, especially as a 'backbone'. The flowers open gradually and the dead ones can be removed. Sometimes the tip is very long; these buds are unlikely to open and can be removed if wayward, although some arrangers like a curved tip. Obtainable most of the year.

Heather; Erica; obtainable in winter and spring. Small flowers in pink, red, purple or white, sometimes bi-coloured, woody, strong stems. Heather will dry in an arrangement so buy it when you see it in the shops and then it can be used all winter for designs. No special treatment except to slit the end of the woody stem.

Ixia; six-petalled, star-shaped flowers borne at the top of wiry stems, useful for small arrangements. The colours are yellows, white flushed red, red, purple, blue usually with dark or light centres. Obtainable in summer, no special treatment.

Lilium; many species and some, such as *Lilium longiflorum,* can be found all year in shops although the greatest choice is available in summer. These elegant, dramatic, large flowers are extremely beautiful in arrangements and can be used singly or with other flowers. No special conditioning but if you wish to avoid yellow and brown stains on your skin and clothing, snip off the pollen-bearing anthers. Blue flowers are not obtainable but there are varieties of all other colours. The stems are often sold by the number of flowers each carries. Stems with only one flower are easier to place in an arrangement. Those with many flowers usually need to be used by themselves or to have some flowers removed, which can be wasteful. The petals should not look crepe-like but should be glistening; the yellow centres should be light in colour.

Mimosa is so pretty but short-lived, so the problem is how to make mimosa last. It is now sold in a polythene bag to conserve moisture. Retain this until you arrange the flowers. However, I have found that mimosa will dry in one day in an arrangement, but when dry will last for many days and still look attractive, though not as full and light in colour.

Orchid; usually extremely long-lasting and although expensive initially they are worth the cost in vase-life. Many very beautiful species and colours, large and small flowers, sometimes on single stems, usually in sprays. The florist will normally cut off a single flower, but this will have a short stem. Orchids are not easy to arrange with other flowers and are often used in a specimen vase or with foliage and driftwood. No special treatment.

Protea; sometimes imported, and a good buy as many will dry gradually and can be used indefinitely. The strong, woody stems need no special treatment. Showy flowers, especially the huge 'king' *protea,* usually surrounded with numerous coloured stiff bracts.

Roses, rosa; are the most difficult of florist's flowers to prevent from wilting. But the smaller varieties, such as 'Carol', 'Belinda' and similar, are especially long lasting.

It is important to remove most of the foliage and to cut the stems shorter when you arrive home. Burn the stem ends in a gas or match flame for one-half to one minute and then place at once in a receptacle of deep, tepid water. At the same time place the flowers in a cool, dim room for 24 hours before arranging them. Some flower arrangers stand the stem ends in 2 inches (5cm) of boiling water instead of charring them, but the flower heads must be protected from the steam. If a rose does flop in an arrangement, float the whole stem and flower on tepid water for a few hours, after which is should revive.

Scabious should have a light green and not a fluffy centre and will then be very long-lasting.

Strawflower, Helichrysum bracteatum; often found in bunches in autumn and should be bought if you do not grow this annual everlasting. It dries as it grows and can be used indefinitely. (See Chapter 7 for adding a wire stem.) Orange, yellow, red, pink, and white flowers. The stems can be used in an arrangement when fresh as they are reasonably stout but they will eventually shrivel. The flowers do not.

Strelitzia, bird-of-paradise; exotic, expensive flowers which can last at least a month, with green, purple-flushed bracts from which emerge a succession of long, keeled, orange and blue flowers in an erect position. The stems are very strong and no special treatment is necessary, but if the flowers die and another does not emerge from the bract, ease it out gently and pull off the dead flowers. Usually found in early summer in shops but can sometimes be ordered especially. Often called 'birds' by florists.

Sweet william, Dianthus barbatus; densely packed, flattened flower heads, sold in bunches in summer. Strong stems and many colours in white or red, marked with other colours.

GARDEN FLOWERS

Flowers cut from the garden need extra treatment because they have not had the benefit of the florist's attention.

Cutting

Cut at any time in cool or rainy weather, but on warm, dry days avoid cutting in the middle of the day when the plant contains less water. In the early morning the plant contains the most water so it should be cut then. If this is not possible, evening is the next best time because the plant then contains the maximum food reserves; cuttings can be placed in water overnight, in a cool place, before being arranged.

It is advisable, although not always practical, to cut stems and place them immediately into a bucket containing several inches of tepid water carried around the garden as you cut. Flower scissors or a sharp knife are the best tools for cutting.

Roses, hydrangeas and rhododendrons benefit from being floated in a bath of tepid water for a few hours after cutting. Wrapping flowers in wet newspaper is also helpful.

Stem treatment

Stems of plants vary; they can be soft, hard, woody or hollow. They can also contain latex. Each type of stem needs slightly different preparation.

Soft (such as gladioli). No preparation needed, other than recutting the stem end if it has been out of water.

Float a wilting rose on tepid water for several hours

You can char the stem end of a florist's rose by holding it in a gas or match flame

Hard (such as roses). Recut the stem and slit up for about 1 inch (2.5cm) to help water absorption. Hold the stem ends over a gas, match or candle flame until blackened, or put them in 2 inches (5cm) of very hot water and stand in a cool place for an hour or two as you would for florist's roses. Protect the flower heads by placing them well to one side of the receptacle or by covering them with thin paper or a roomy polythene bag or a light-weight absorbent cloth.

Woody (such as hydrangeas). Recut and slit, and scrape 2 inches (5cm) of bark off the stem end.

Hollow (such as delphiniums). Upturn the flower and fill the stem with water, plugging the end with a tissue or cotton wool which acts as a wick and continues to draw up water.

Stems which leak (such as poppies). Hold the stem ends over a gas, match or candle flame until blackened. Charring makes the latex already exuded more permeable.

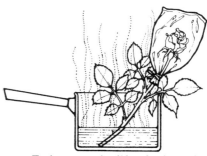

To increase the life of a florist's rose, treat stem end of rose by standing in 2 inches (5cm) of very hot water, keeping flower head protected or away from steam

Removing leaves

Some delicate flowers should have all the leaves on their stems removed so that the water travels to the flowers only. Mock orange, buddleia, lilac, laburnum, clematis and bells-of-Ireland should be defoliated completely, and also any other flowers that seem delicate and of a thin texture such as harebells or poppies, or which have many leaves on their stems, such as long-stemmed florist's roses which should have most of the leaves removed. The greater the surface area, the more water will evaporate. But cutting down the number of leaves, less water will be lost.

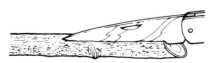

Treat woody stem end by recutting and slitting up for about 1 inch (2.5cm) to help water absorption

Fill hollow stems with water and plug with cotton wool

Grooming

Damaged flowers and leaves should be removed at this stage and also any foliage that would be under water when arranged in the vase.

Conditioning

This is a term used generally for the preparation of stems and their subsequent soaking, in a cool place. Unlike florist's flowers it is necessary to fill up the stems of garden flowers with water before arranging them. This is best achieved by placing the stem ends in a bucket about half-full of tepid water and placing this in a cool, dim place. After a few hours the stems should be turgid and ready for placing in an arrangement.

GARDEN FLOWERS REQUIRING SPECIAL TREATMENT

Alliums: avoid using hot water because, as mentioned, this increases the onion smell.

Berries: spray with hair lacquer for some protection from water loss. Try some glycerine in the vase water.

Bougainvilleas: submerge overnight after defoliating.

Bulrushes: spray with hair lacquer to avoid seeds loosening and blowing away.

Camellias: spray the air around the flower with water because the woody stems do not take up water quickly.

Clematis: submerge for an hour after defoliating, but they are usually difficult to condition.

Coleus foliage: do not submerge as it spoils the colour but the stem ends will often root in water.

Euphorbias: char the stem ends and avoid getting the latex in or near your eyes as it can be very harmful.

Gardenias: the flowers mark easily and the petals should not be touched by hand.

Gerberas: remove 2 inches (5cm) of stem and burn the ends.

Hellebores: the only flowers that seem to defy all the experts until in the seed stage when they will last for days.

Hemerocallis (day-lilies): the flowers only last a day but dead flowers can be cut off and any buds left to open next day.

Hibiscus: one-day flowers that last as well out of water as in.

Holly berries: cut several weeks before Christmas because otherwise the birds may have eaten them. Place the branches in a bucket half-full of water and in a cool place or out-of-doors; cover with a polythene bag pulled down over the sides. The protected berries become quite plump.

Hydrangeas: the coloured 'petals' are flower-like bracts. They can be submerged for about two hours. But the secret is to cut mature flowers that have become slightly papery. These will dry in the arrangement for winter use. If you use young flowers spray them well or place damp tissue paper on them overnight.

Kale: avoid hot water which increases the cabbage smell.

Laburnum: defoliate, but these flowers last only a day or two.

Lilies: remove the anthers with flower scissors if you wish to avoid yellow stains.

Mimosa: keep in the polythene bag until arranged. Spray well.

Molucella laevis (bells-of-Ireland): defoliate and add glycerine to the water.

Philadelphus: defoliate.

Passion flowers: one-day flowers that should be defoliated and floated on water.

Poinsettias: these Christmas flowers belong to the *Euphorbia* family and the cut ends must be well charred.

Stephanotis: the flowers can turn brown if touched by water.

Strelitzias: these may appear dead after a few days but further flowers can be eased out of the enclosing sheath to give several weeks of life.

Violets: these flowers live naturally in damp places and their petals are very tolerant of water. For longer life upturn a bunch overnight in a saucer of water.

Zinnias: the necks flop easily and a stub wire pushed up the stem can prevent this.

AFTERCARE OF FLOWER ARRANGEMENTS

There is a tendency to use small containers and small blocks of Oasis for many flowers, which means the water is used up quickly. Flowers last longer in deep water. As the water evaporates it provides a beneficial moist atmosphere around the flowers. It also needs less topping up.

I try to avoid using Oasis (or water-retaining foam with other trade names) for a large arrangement in warm weather. It is amazing how quickly the foam dries out; it needs watering on the surface at least once a day, and should stand in water. Also, I do not use a small container because this needs topping up too frequently for a large number of stems.

Avoid placing flowers in a draught, or in a warm place such as near a television set, open fire or radiator, or a light, sunny window. Cool, dimly lit positions are better for the long life of flowers.

Additives to the water

There are many old wives' tales about pennies, alcohol and so on, but one that has proved true is aspirin — when there are

27 A small container must be topped up often and the flowers well-sprayed. (*Arranger* Joan Ewing)

45

Spray plant material with fine mist spray to reduce transpiration from both leaves and flowers

many leaves in an arrangement (for full details see Chapter 4). Use half a soluble aspirin to a pint of water. Half a teaspoonful of a mild disinfectant is also helpful, and avoids having to change the vase water.

Spraying

Providing plenty of water for the stem ends is only half the answer to maintaining vase-life. In a warm room or hot weather it is advisable to spray an arrangement with a mister every day. This creates a moist atmosphere around the flowers. If you remove an arrangement overnight to a cool place and spray it you will be surprised how fresh it will be next day. In the summer church flowers last better than those in homes because they are in a cooler atmosphere.

TRANSPORTING FLOWERS

A bunch of cut flowers carried in a warm hand, and unprotected, can wilt quickly. A few flowers can be carried in a polythene bag tied at the bottom. This holds in the moisture. A lot of flowers can be transported in a cardboard flower box lined with thin polythene after the normal conditioning (see page 43). Cover the flowers with the polythene wrapping and replace the lid.

If flowers are required to travel for more than a day, place soaked J-cloths over the stems and foliage but not over the petals which can mark. Stem ends can also be wrapped in soaked cotton-wool (freesias are often sold in this way). If the weather is especially hot, try to keep the boxes out of the sun and get them into a cool place as quickly as possible.

QUICK HINTS

Buy good quality flowers in bud.
Hold the stem ends of flowers in a gas or match flame.
Place the stems immediately afterwards in deep tepid water.
Remove the receptacle to a cool, dimly-lit position for 24 hours.
Keep stem ends under water whenever possible.
Clean all utensils, containers and tools.
Keep flower arrangements away from hot or draughty positions.
Increase the humidity around flowers by spraying lightly.
Choose a container that holds enough water in proportion to the number of stems in an arrangement. This is difficult to determine because the room in which the arrangement is placed may be dry or cool, and different flowers require different amounts of water. Experience will eventually indicate the amount of water necessary. Slide a finger down into the container to feel the water level and top up when the water level drops an inch or more in a deep container. If you have to top up daily, then the container is too small for the number of stems.

SOME EXPLANATIONS

Why must cut stems have water?

Water is a vital constituent of living matter and in the case of plants keeps the tissues turgid. In some plants water is sometimes responsible for supporting the plant, although those with rigid stem tissue have additional support. Water is necessary for the stem ends because the tubes in the stem are cut at this point and take up water. In the growing plant water is drawn up, because of transpiration, through the roots and stems to the leaves and flowers.

In addition to taking up water through the cut stem ends precious moisture can be conserved by keeping damp air around flowers and leaves, using a mister.

What is transpiration?

Anything wet loses its moisture to the surrounding air if the air is drier. For example wet clothes dry quickly on a dry, windy day. In the same way the petals of flowers and leaves lose moisture to the surrounding air in a dry room. This is called transpiration. As they do this they draw up the water they are standing in through their stem ends. Flowers wilt when the water in the container (or water-retaining foam) runs out and also if the rate at which the petals and leaves lose water exceeds the amount taken up through the stems. This happens with flowers that have many petals such as large roses.

How can you stop a flower arrangement wilting?

This can be avoided by having plenty of water for the stem ends and by spraying a mist of water over the arrangement from time to time. This is one of the best ways of counteracting wilting, but it is not often used, except by experienced flower arrangers.

Why do high temperatures cause wilting?

High temperatures and draughts mean increased evaporation from all moist surfaces and rapid transpiration.

Why do cool temperatures revive flowers?

Transpiration is cut down when plants are in cool temperatures, and in the dark, which is the reason for conditioning and reviving flowers in a cool, dim place.

Why use a mild disinfectant?

One of the major factors responsible for the wilting of a cut flower is blockage of the cut end of the stem with bacteria that grow around the minute water tubes. A mild disinfectant discourages the growth. But avoid using a strong disinfectant which may harm the flowers.

Why keep containers clean?

It is advisable to keep containers, flower scissors, mechanics and buckets very clean. They can be washed with water containing detergent and bleach if necessary, and well rinsed afterwards. The reason is that otherwise bacteria will grow more

easily. Metal containers, and charcoal or a mild disinfectant a
a water additive, help to keep water odourless and clean. Th
water-retaining foams (Oasis and other trade names) contain
formaldehyde which restricts bacterial activity.

Why remove leaves below water?

Many leaves decay quickly when under water for more than .
few hours, and this also encourages bacterial growth. Some
leaves, such as those on chrysanthemums, deteriorate more
quickly than others and soon become slimy.

What is an air-lock?

Recut stems under water to prevent
air locks

If a stem is left out of water the column of water normally
travelling up the stem stops. Air can then enter the stem and
cause a block, in the same way as bacteria can block the water
carrying tubes. This is the reason for placing cut stems in a
bucket of water as soon as they are cut and for recutting stem
ends that have been out of water for some time. Flower
should be arranged in a container that already holds some
water. Burning the stem ends can help to remove most of the
air. And so can boiling water if you stand the stem end in abou
2 inches (5cm) of water, protecting the flower heads with a
light cloth or tissue paper. Recutting a stem end under water
also removes air bubbles. This is especially beneficial to car
nations, pinks, gerberas, marigolds, sweet peas, chrysanthemum
and snapdragons, according to experiments.

Can a seal form on a stem end?

In the same way that our skin starts to heal after we have cut it
a seal forms on the cut end of a stem when it has been out of
water for some time. The recutting of a stem end removes
any seal; so does boiling water and charring with a flame.

Why not hammer stem ends?

Smashing the stem ends with a hammer tends to damage the
tissues and can encourage decay. Also a smashed stem end is
difficult to impale on a pinholder or push into Oasis. A clean
slit using a knife or flower scissors is much better and increases
water absorption.

Why char leaking stem ends?

Stems that bleed latex stop the uptake of water. Fluid comes
down rather than being taken up. Charring the stem ends stops
this leakage.

What can be done to lengthen the lives of cut flowers?

Experiments on additives to lengthen vase-life must be made
under carefully controlled conditions. For example, the flowers
to be compared should be of the same age, placed in the same
temperature and container and given equal amounts of water.
It is difficult for the average flower arranger to do this at home.
However experiments are being conducted, especially by the
cut flower trade. Commercial preparations containing nutrients
and a mild disinfectant can be bought to increase vase-life.

Why do some flowers wilt more quickly than others?

Some plants have natural protection from water loss. This is specially true of cacti and succulents, which grow in naturally hot, dry conditions. Evergreens have greater protection against water loss than deciduous trees; aspidistras, monsteras, yucca and ivy tolerate lack of moisture. It must be accepted that some flowers, such as thin-tissued wild flowers, have very little protection and will wilt at once. Young leaves will wilt quickly because they rely on water to hold their shape until they have stronger tissue.

The entire surface of a young plant is covered by a layer of cells known as the epidermis. The outer walls of the epidermal cells have a waterproof material in and over them, differing in thickness from plant to plant. Plants growing in regions where water is scarce have a thicker waterproof covering than those growing where water is more plentiful. Older parts of plants normally grow a protective layer of cork to replace the epidermis. It differs according to the plant but is waterproof to varying extents.

Why is tepid water advisable?

Warm water moves more easily than cold water and when it is important to maintain a flow of water up a stem to avoid the top wilting, the sooner water gets up the stem the better. Boiling water is even more 'runny', but can destroy the stem end and make it floppy. Steam can also harm the flowers.

Can you stop needled evergreens from dropping?

This is difficult because the needles dry out so quickly. A moist atmosphere helps as does adding a tablespoonful of glycerine to a pint of vase water.

Is it better to hold a stem in a flame than in boiling water?

It has the same effect but is more drastic. The heat kills the cells and stops them growing into a protective seal or callous. The large area of dead cells allows water to enter the stem end more easily. It also slows down the leakage of sap that causes bacterial growth. Many flower arrangers like the charring treatment because it helps to get rid of seals and air bubbles, coagulates proteins in cells and lessens the living barrier to water movement and sterilises the stem end.

Can you retard the development of flowers?

Sometimes you may wish to have flowers for a special occasion but need to buy them ahead of time. If you stand flowers in water in a cold (though not freezing) dark place their growth is retarded. Peonies and gladioli can be left out of water on a cold floor for some days; recut the stem ends before placing in tepid water when you wish to start their development again. Flowers can be placed in the refrigerator, but not the freezer. This is a suitable treatment for corsages and single flowers with the stem end in a tube of water. The flowers should be enclosed in a polythene bag or box.

4 FOLIAGE ARRANGEMENTS

28 Aspidistra leaves will last for weeks and the flowers can be changed for dahlias or carnations; roses or chrysanthemums could also be used. Fatshedera or ivy leaves hide the mechanics and grapes add another shape, but leaves could be used in their place in the container. (*Arranger* Dorothy Haworth)

One of the most interesting developments in recent years ha been the decorative use of cut foliage as well as cut flowers In paintings of earlier flower arrangements leaves appear only when attached to the stems of flowers, and rarely seem to have been included for their own value. But now leaves are being used more and more, alone or combined with flowers.

But they are still underrated for decorative arrangement and one wonders why. Perhaps the narrow title of the subjec 'flower arrangement', which now incorporates all types o plant material, is the reason; people feel that flowers must be included. Or maybe the brilliant colours of flowers are so dominant that they catch our eyes first. It could be just a matter of habit to cut or buy flowers and to think of a lea as a mere filler of an odd space, instead of beautiful plant material in its own right.

If you have some leaves, you can have an arrangement in your home and at little expense – many of the leaves last very well when cut and certainly longer than most flowers. I have known aspidistra, ivy and some evergreens to last for many weeks in an arrangement, even to the extent of rooting in the container.

Foliage is very versatile. It can be cut on long branches for linear beauty or with short stems for concealing mechanics it can be used as a background for flowers, as an outline, in a pattern and in any style – traditional, landscape, modern or abstract. It can look elegant, dramatic, dainty, elaborate, exotic, simple, rigid, curved and so on.

SOURCES OF SUPPLY

If you have a garden it is important to introduce plants with useful foliage for arrangements. But you may be surprised on looking around how many useful leaves already grow in your garden. Furthermore, you can have leaves all the year round; evergreens are many and most gardens have a few for brightening the winter months. If I had a small garden I would grow plants for foliage rather than flowers, which can always be bought in variety all year.

If you have no garden, you will find that florists now stock foliage as well as flowers. You can also glycerine leaves gleaned during the summer in the countryside when you cannot find fresh foliage (see Chapter 7). Nurserymen will sometimes cut foliage for you if available, but do order it in advance because they are busy people and it takes time to cut foliage. Even houseplants can yield a leaf or two, but I am always reluctant to cut these and can usually find another source of supply.

In the countryside there are often huge beech, holly, larch, fir and other trees which do not miss an odd branch. And there are wild carrot leaves in damp places. Young sycamore leaves are a beautiful bronze colour and grow out of the base of the tree trunk. It does no harm to cut anything in moderation where it is plentiful. Remember, however, that it is an offence to pick anything on private land and in parks and nature reserves.

LEAF SHAPES

John Ruskin wrote, 'Leaves take on all kinds of strange shapes as if to invite us to examine them.' There is more variety of shape in leaves than there is in flowers. They can be heart-shaped like an anthurium leaf, star-shaped like those of some begonias and *Fatsia japonica,* indented like those of a Swiss cheese plant, circular like a series of coins on a branch of eucalyptus, tall and dignified like New Zealand flax, round like a geranium leaf, elegant as aspidistra, even pleated like veratrum or currugated like peperomia.

Leaves grow singly and in sprays, with or without branches, which can be curved and graceful as in camellia, or straight as in forsythia. Leaves grow upwards, sideways and downwards and we can arrange them in these positions; for example, ivy and honeysuckle for cascades and trails. Some leaves grow in a cluster at the top of a stem, radiating like the spokes of a wheel, as in mahonia. Others grow opposite each other and some alternately. Once you begin to think of variations, they seem endless. The only rhythm of growth that is not prevalent enough is a rosette shape which is only found in a few plants like the houseleek or London pride foliage.

LEAF COLOURS

We normally think of foliage as green and perhaps this is one of the reasons why we do not make enough foliage arrangements; we may think there is not enough colour in them. But taking a look around a garden or a nursery you can find blue, grey and yellow greens, dark and light greens. Often the green is variegated, spotted or splashed with another colour. Sometimes the underside of the leaf is quite different, or there are patterns of another colour.

Apart from the many greens available there are bronzes, browns, reds, yellows, silvers, greys, purples, either alone or mixed as in the resplendent croton. In the autumn changing leaf colourings vie with the colours of flowers everywhere.

The most usual fault in a foliage arrangement is the use of one shade of green only; try adding a blue-green and a yellow green to a mid-green and the design comes immediately to life. Once you become conscious of the tremendous variety of shape and colour in leaves you will enjoy a new awareness and find making an all-foliage arrangement very easy and satisfying.

TEXTURES

In addition to a variety of shape and colour there are many leaf textures — shiny, glossy, dull, velvety, woolly, rough and smooth. Sometimes the textures on the back and the front of a leaf are different. In addition to looking for several shades of green, try to find a variety of textures because this adds interest.

LONG-LIVED LEAVES

Green leaves are perforated with many stomata or pores, which are microscopic-sized openings with guard cells to control them. At night they close and moisture remains in the leaves, but in the light hours they open to absorb carbon dioxide and proceed with normal growth. This means they lose water by evaporation to the surrounding air. This is called transpiration. The more leaves on the stem the more water is lost.

Preparation

Scrape the bark from the outside of woody stem ends for about 2 inches (5cm) and slit up hard and woody stems for about 1 inch (2.5cm) so that they can absorb water more easily (see page 43). The majority of leaves are prepared (usually called conditioning) by submerging them under tepid water or floating them on top of water for a few hours. Grey and silver leaves are the exception because the colour is caused by many tiny hairs; once these become waterlogged they look green and also drip in the arrangement.

This immersion lessens transpiration and the cells become fully charged with water. If the leaves are to travel later without water then it is best to pack them in a polythene bag to retain the moisture. Thicker leaves contain far more moisture than thin ones, and so last longer.

Leaves decay quickly if left under water for more than a few hours and so it is advisable to remove the foliage from the part of the stem that will be submerged in the container of water.

29 A long-lasting arrangement of ivies, yucca and driftwood. The variegated ivy adds life to the design. (*Arranger* Edith Brack)

Additives

During the light hours leaves in an arrangement can lose more water through transpiration than they can take up from the container of water This causes wilting and vase-life is shortened. Half a soluble aspirin dissolved in a pint of water is excellent for increasing the life of foliage arrangements, as reliable experiments have proved recently. A low aspirin concentration keeps the stomata almost closed during the light hours and so less water is lost. The fact that this slows down growth is no disadvantage in a cut leaf.

With long-lived foliage arrangements it is advisable to add disinfectant to the vase water, for half a teaspoonful of a mild disinfectant will discourage the growth of bacteria, which can block the cut ends of stems and cause an unpleasant smell.

Moist air

The humidity of the atmosphere around an arrangement also affects the life of foliage. If it is dry because of draught or heat then transpiration occurs at a faster rate, but if the atmosphere is moist it is slowed up. Humans do not like living in a damp atmosphere so it helps the foliage arrangement to live longer if it is given a mini-atmosphere of moist air. This can be provided by spraying water on the leaves, especially underneath, every few days with a fine mister obtainable from a garden centre or florist. Removing the arrangement to a cool place overnight and spraying will certainly lengthen life and is well worthwhile during winter when rooms are drier.

A simple foliage arrangement in which water is also featured so that the 'pool' of water evaporates near the leaves, also provides a moist atmosphere.

DESIGN

Collect foliage with varying shapes, textures and colours. It should all be in scale.

Traditional arrangements

Branches and long leaves can be used for height; short-stemmed, flat leaves like those of a geranium or a bergenia can be inserted into the mechanics at a sideways angle to conceal them; other interesting shapes and colours can be used elsewhere.

The shape that we are short of in foliage is a rosette, a shape similar to a circular flower. In traditional designs we have become so used to forming a 'centre of interest' with rounded flowers in the middle, that we often come to a full stop when trying to find a centre for a foliage arrangement. Houseleeks, London Pride, succulents and kale are a useful circular shape. A cluster of laurel is effective or a cluster can be made by grouping several leaves together. Alternatively the arrangement can be made predominantly of foliage with two or three

30 *Elagnus pungens* 'Aurea maculata' has green, yellow-splashed leaves and is a long-lasting evergreen. The woody stems need splitting and scraping. The yellow dahlias can easily be replaced in the foliage framework which also includes fatshedera. Apples and grapes give variety of shape. (*Arranger* Molly Duerr)

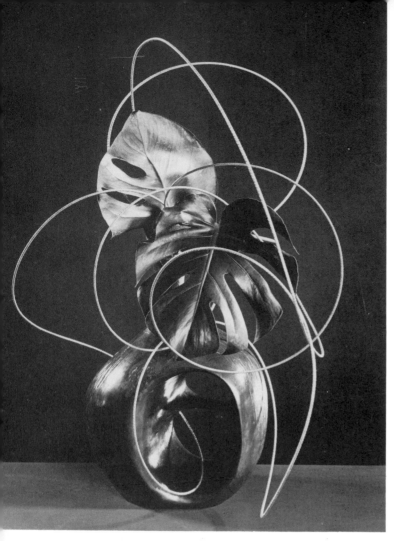

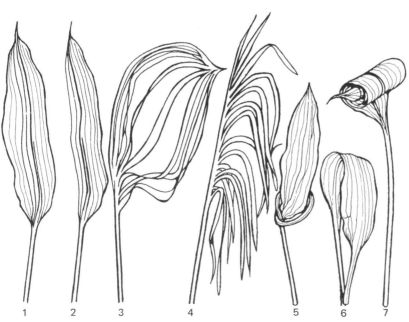

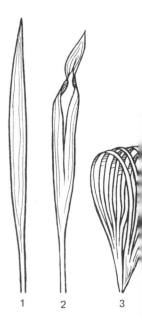

1 2 3   4   5 6 7   1 2 3

1 *Opposite left* A modern arrangement of cane and two leaves of *Monstera deliciosa* (Swiss cheese plant). (*Arranger* Marian Aronson)

2 *Opposite right* Two trimmed *Fatsia japonica* leaves with stems for a long lasting decorative design. (*Arranger* Edith Brack)

33 *Below right* Blue cedar has beautiful curves which make a graceful framework for the figurine. Flowers can be used instead of the figurine. Cedar should be sprayed with water occasionally. (*Arranger* Molly Duerr)

Below left Aspidistra leaf:
1. Natural form   2. Broad side trimmed with scissors   3. Inner surface shredded with thumbnail   4. One side shredded with thumbnail   5. Tied leaf   6. Leaf furled and stem placed over its tip   7. Leaf furled and pinned or stapled

Below New Zealand Flax:
1. Natural form   2. Split down the centre and turned inside out   3. Shredded with thumbnail and looped   4. Tip threaded through short splits in the leaf   5. Shredded with thumbnail or razor blade   6. Formed into a simple loop

4   5   6

rounded flowers arranged as a centre of interest. This is certainly not an expensive use of flowers and they can be changed as they fade, leaving the foliage in position.

Landscape designs

These are arrangements which exactly repeat nature in a realistic manner, but all the components are scaled down. Branches and leaves follow the pattern of natural growth and a twig becomes 'a tree'.

Modern arrangements

There is more restraint and an emphasis on space in which to see unusual forms and contrasting textures. Often only two or three leaves of each variety will be used and only two varieties such as tall leaves like iris for height and oval shapes such as hosta for contrast.

Abstract

In abstract designs a leaf is used as designing material and its habit of growth is not regarded. Often only one variety of leaf is used. Foliage is slit, cut, twisted, curved, bent, shredded and looped by the designer to gain a desired effect.

Long lasting leaves

Plant name classification	Leaf shape, colour, stem	Use in design	Source	Treatment and comments
Anthurium (evergreen)	heart-shaped or oval, dark green, up to 7in., 8in. or 24in long, stems 6-18in.	dramatic for modern styles when shape can be seen	greenhouse, florist, houseplant	spray or wipe off dust
Aspidistra lurida cast-iron plant (evergreen)	graceful, arching, oblong with pointed tips, narrowing to the hard stem, up to about 14in. long, dark green, or white striped	modern or traditional styles; can be split, curled, shredded for abstract designs	greenhouse, houseplant	will dry out to tan colour in an arrangement; preserving with glycerine gives better results; spray or wipe dust off leaves while green
Aucuba japonica 'Variegata' spotted laurel (hardy, evergreen shrub)	narrow, oval, bright green, mottled gold; short stems; on a main stem can look rosette-shaped	modern or traditional, good for concealing mechanics or forming a centre of interest in a foliage design	garden, patio pot, houseplant	soak two hours in tepid water, spray
Bergenia elephant's ear (hardy perennial evergreen ground cover)	circular, spoon-shaped or oval, on 3-10in. long or short stems, green sometimes red-edged, changing in autumn to flame and yellow	indispensable for flower arrangers for concealing mechanics and providing a plain background for flowers, modern or traditional	garden	soak two hours in tepid water, spray
Buxus box (evergreen shrub)	green or green blotched yellow, or white, glossy, small, oval, opposite on the stems which are woody	for small traditional designs and good filler for cones, 'topiary' trees and garlands	florist, garden	will keep for months in polythene bag so preparations for special decorations can be made ahead
Camellia japonica (generally hardy evergreen tree or shrub)	glossy, dark green leaves broadly oval and pointed, 3-4in. long, woody stem	traditional designs, some times in modern, good for outline or as a filler	garden, florist, greenhouse	split and scrape stems, lasts for months when cut

Plant name classification	Leaf shape, colour, stem	Use in design	Source	Treatment and comments
Chamaecyparis (hardy evergreen coniferous tree)	foliage flattened in sprays in one plane, with leaves in small overlapping scales, blue-green, yellows, silver-grey, bronze, bright green, variegations	good filler in traditional designs, though can look fussy, excellent for garlands, swags and so on for Christmas decorations	garden, florist	can be cut several weeks in advance and left on damp ground; will last two weeks without moisture for garlands
Choisya ternata Mexican orange (evergreen shrub)	glossy, 'fingered' leaves in rosettes on woody stems	for outline if well trimmed, traditional designs, some modern; can make a centre for a foliage design	garden	remove young foliage which wilts, otherwise lasts months
Clivia (leek-like plant, not hardy)	strap-shaped, dark green glossy, up to 24in. long, without stems	useful for modern and abstract styles	florist, greenhouse	soak two hours in tepid water, cut leaf base to a point to insert in mechanics
Cupressus macrocarpa (evergreen conifer)	plume-like branchlets of foliage with closely pressed rather fleshy scales, yellow, dark green	as for *Chamaecyparis*	garden, florist	as for *Chamaecyparis*
Curtonus paniculatus (cormous plant)	pleated blades, four or five to the stem, 2½ft long, mid-green	good height, modern or traditional	garden	soak two hours, may turn brown at tips, will dry in arrangements
Cytisus Broom (deciduous mainly, a few evergreen shrubs)	grey-green or dark green foliage, insignificant, small on arching green branches which are very pliable	outline in traditional designs, for dramatic sweeps in modern styles	garden	avoid young growth, branches can be tied in curves and soaked for two hours to provide excellent curved branches which will dry in the arrangement
Echeveria (greenhouse perennial succulent)	rosettes of thick, fleshy leaves, often with a white, waxy sheen, pale green, pale mauve, blue-green	one of the few rosette shapes in foliage, useful for centres of designs, modern or traditional	greenhouse, houseplant	needs little water and can be used out of water for several weeks; be careful to avoid knocking off outer leaves, can be used with root attached and then replanted

Plant name classification	Leaf shape, colour, stem	Use in design	Source	Treatment and comments
Elaeagnus (hardy, evergreen shrub, a few are deciduous)	leathery, oval leaves up to 4in. long on woody branches, silvery surface on the underside, plain green or green splashed yellow on upper surface	good outline plant material for traditional arrangements, also useful filler, suitable for large arrangements when long branches are cut	garden	scrape and split the woody stems, spray
Escallonia (evergreen shrub, slightly tender)	dark green, glossy oval, small on hard stems, many to a branch, long shoots	useful outline plant material for traditional designs	garden	split the stems, spray
Eucalyptus gunnii gum tree (evergreen tree or shrub)	round young leaves up to 2½in. diameter, becoming oval later, blue-green to grey, almost lilac, leaves grow opposite in pairs	outline or filler for traditional designs	florist, garden	will dry in an arrangement
Euonymus spindle tree (shrub or climber, evergreen, some deciduous)	*E. fortunei* 'variegata' is a good climber with small leaves edged white, tinged pink in winter, oval shape, many to a woody stem. *E. japonicus* 'aureo-picta', a shrub, has green leaves blotched yellow and shiny, woody stems	adds colour variation, good filler plant material for traditional designs, also could be outline plant material	garden	split and scrape woody stems
Fatsia japonica (evergreen shrub)	exceptionally large palmate leaves in mid-green, ranging from 5-15 in. in diameter, turn yellow-brown in old age; stems vary in about the same proportion as the leaf diameter	indispensable for large designs and for modern styles, excellent for concealing mechanics in pedestal style arrangements	garden	soak two hours, spray, lasts weeks

Plant name classification	Leaf shape, colour, stem	Use in design	Source	Treatment and comments
Galax aphylla wand plant (evergreen)	tough, shiny, circular leaves, dark green with band of crimson when exposed to sun, up to 5in. in diameter, wiry stalks	covers mechanics well and is an excellent background for flowers; a rosette can be made for the centre of an arrangement	garden, American florists	no special treatment, lasts weeks
Gaultheria shallon (evergreen shrub, ground cover)	Broadly oval or slightly heart-shaped, rough-textured, leathery leaves about 2-3in, very dark green	useful for concealing mechanics and as a plain background for flowers	garden	lasts weeks when cut
Griselinia littoralis (evergreen shrub)	oval, tough, leathery, light green leaves on woody stems	outline or filler plant material	garden	no special conditioning
Hedera ivy (hardy evergreen climber)	ovate or heart-shaped usually, green, green with yellow or grey or cream, yellow stems woody but leaf stems softer	single, larger leaves for hiding mechanics and as plain backing for flowers, branches as trailers; modern and traditional styles	garden, hedgerow	single leaves are easier to place in mechanics when a stitch of wire is made across the central vein and wound round the stem for strength
Helleborus corsicus Corsican hellebore (evergreen, hardy perennial)	three-lobed, mid- to pale grey green, thick and spiny, waxy texture, shortish stems	filler material not solid enough to conceal mechanics, for traditional styles	garden	the best hellebore foliage for cutting
Hosta Plantain lily (hardy perennial, ground cover)	broad single leaves, many varieties of different sizes in ovals or heart shape, sometimes wavy, green, blue-green, green with white or yellow, stems vary in length	all hostas are useful as fillers, as background flowers and hiding mechanics and as outline material, useful in modern or traditional designs	garden	soak for two hours before arranging, will dry gradually in an arrangement

Plant name (classification)	Leaf shape, colour, stem	Use in design	Source	Treatment and comment
Iris pallida but most iris leaves are useful (hardy perennial)	sword-shaped in a fan usually, green with yellow or white or plain green	provide height and a 'back-bone' for an arrangement, usually in modern style, naturalistic or abstract	garden	cut the base of the leaf to a point for inserting into Oasis
Magnolia grandiflora (hardy evergreen tree)	mid to dark green glossy leaves, oval and leathery with rust-coloured felted underside	good single leaves for hiding mech-anics, green or brown side can be used, branches for larger arrange-ments, modern or traditional	garden	no soaking, will dry in the arrangement
Mahonia (evergreen shrub) *Mahonia X* 'Charity' best for flower arrangers	glossy, dark green leaflets, spine-toothed, on each leaf, strong stems on woody branches, leaves often shot with red and yellow when mature in winter, or bronze, leaves arranged in whorls	single leaves are useful fillers, whole branches with long stems also useable for traditional and modern designs	garden, florist for some varieties	cutting a whole whorl does no harm and in fact encourages growth; no special treatment
Palm trachycarpus fortunei (fan palm)	mid-green, pleated fan-shaped leaves about 3ft wide on stalks sharply toothed and up to 3ft long	fan palm can be trimmed to a number of shapes for modern and abstract	greenhouse, holidays in warmer climates, dried in florists	very long-lasting as they will dry in an arrangement
Phoenix dactylifera date palm (evergreens)	mid-green pinnate leaves look feathery, can be up to 6ft long	useful for huge pedestal arrange-ments, tradition-al style, can also be trimmed for modern and abstract styles		

Plant name (classification)	Leaf shape, colour, stem	Use in design	Source	Treatment and comment
Phormium tenax New Zealand flax (evergreen perennial)	single strap shaped leaves up to 10 ft long mid to dark green, variegated with yellow, or bronze-purple, straight and not in graceful curves	useful height for a back-bone in a pedestal or traditional arrangement, and in modern styles, can be bent, slit for abstract styles	garden	very long lasting, dry in an arrangement but curl to pencil thin
Pittosporum tenuifolium (half-hardy evergreen shrub)	small pale green leaves on almost black stems which tend to be rigid	filler for small modern arrangements	warm garden, florists	no special treatment
Rhododendron (evergreen shrub, hardy, can be greenhouse and deciduous)	commonly grown rhododendrons have dark green, oval leaves on woody stems, appearing as a a whorl at the top but with other leaves down the stem	branches can be used for modern and traditional styles, single leaves for hiding mech-anics, rosettes for a centre of interest	garden	spray often to prevent drying and curling up
Sansevieria trifasciata mother-in-law's tongue (evergreen houseplant)	erect, rigid, sword-shaped single leaves up to 18in. long, dark green, mottled grey but 'Laurentii' is green and yellow	good for height in modern styles	greenhouse houseplant	deep water makes the leaves soggy, sometimes advisable to wrap stem ends in thin polythene
Sedum spectabile 'Autumn Joy' ice-plant (hardy perennial)	fleshy blue-green leaves, oval in twos or threes at each node, strong stems	filler foliage for traditional and some-times modern styles	garden	little water needed, long season for cutting, very long-lasting
Skimmia japonica (hardy, evergreen shrub)	pale green, leathery leaves, oval shape with a rosette appearance	good for filler foliage and for centre of interest, conceals mechanics	florist, garden	short soak, spray

Plant name (classification)	Leaf shape, colour, stem	Use in design	Source	Treatment and comment
Strelitzia bird of paradise flower (houseplant, evergreen perennial)	oval, fan foliage on strong stems about 18in. long, leathery, mid-green	good for height in traditional and modern styles, can be shaped for abstract designs	florist, greenhouse	everlasting leaves which dry to fascinating shapes in arrangements
Thuja (hardy evergreen tree, conifer)	flat scales in greens, golds	filler material for traditional styles	florist, garden	a conifer without needles, no conditioning
Tsuga heterophylla Western hemlock (hardy evergreen tree, conifer)	dark green on top surface, silver below, small, parallel-sided leaves in double ranks on woody branches	excellent outline and filler foliage for traditional styles, good for height	garden, florist	can be used on green or silver side, spray
Viburnum rhytidophyllum *Viburnum tinus laurustinus* (evergreen shrubs)	the first listed has deep green, textured, brown undersides, oval, long, narrow leaves; the second oval, dark green, smaller leaves, woody stems	single leaves good for hiding mechanics, branches rather droopy branches useful for small, traditional styles	garden garden, florist	no special treatment
Yucca filamentosa Adam's needle	stiff, erect narrow leaves in dark green with sharp points	for modern and abstract styles, very stiff	garden	no special treatment
Zantedeschia Arum lily (perennial, half-hardy and tender)	narrow when young, opening to arrow-shaped; up to about 12in. long, stems up to 2ft, arched, soft	excellent for modern styles because of varying shapes and sizes	greenhouse, florist, outdoors for *Z. aethiopica* in mild areas	soak two hours in tepid water, spray; ends split easily so bind with wool or small rubber band

5 FRUIT ARRANGEMENTS

The brilliant colours of fruits and vegetables piled up on market stalls have great fascination — especially in foreign markets where there are unusual products with strange shapes, patterns and textures. Almost any greengrocer can make his display attractive simply by placing fruits and vegetables in grouped patterns. And the stands displaying them at flower shows attract many viewers who marvel at the way they are arranged in concentric circles, huge cones and so on.

All this means that the potential for pattern-making in fruit and vegetables is enormous and for this reason they can be used most decoratively in a home, arranged alone or combined with flowers and leaves. They look especially attractive in a dining room on the table or sideboard.

However home decorations of fruits should not look like a fruit stall or shop window and some thought should be given to the way they are arranged and their colours, shapes and textures combined. I like fruits for arrangements because of their dual purpose; they can be enjoyed in an arrangement and then eaten. Sometimes the family eat them before they have been fully enjoyed in a decoration but they can be easily replaced.

Apart from fruits bought for consumption, there are also many ornamental fruits, including berries, in gardens and countryside. These make beautiful additions to arrangements of autumn leaves and flowers.

EDIBLE FRUIT AND VEGETABLES

My greengrocer is now used to me choosing my own fruit for arrangements, which can be a little different from selecting them just for consumption. Although one does not want to delay trade, most assistants usually enter into the fun of it. Choose unblemished, under-ripe fruit; any ripe fruit ready for eating will soon be of no use in a decoration. Buying under-ripe fruit is like buying flowers in bud — both are chosen to last longer.

I also look for fruit with lovely colour variations such as mangoes with red and orange, a pepper or an apple with both

34 Green and brown grapes, red and green apples, yellow and black plums with foliage of beech, aspidistra, ferns, glycerined sweet chestnut, *monbretia* with dried *verbascum* and hollyhock seedheads. The larger fruits are placed towards the centre of the design and there are lovely contrasts of shape and texture. (*Arranger* Dorothy Berisford)

63

red and green, a lemon or an orange with a touch of green, melons which are partially yellow, peaches of pink and red. I also look for pineapples with undamaged, handsome leaves at the top, for too often these are cut off. Although fruit is seasonal there are many varieties to be found all the year round.

Avoid cut fruit — it deteriorates rapidly and attracts insects when used in an arrangement.

Shapes

Fruit usually has strong structure and bold forms, and it is difficult to make a dainty fruit arrangement. There are many round forms that need softening with other forms, flowers or foliage to break up the solidarity.

The shapes of fruits and vegetables fall into fairly well defined groups for design purposes:

Bulky
Melons, pineapples (edible and the decorative pink variety), cabbages (red and green), small pumpkins, large gourds, squash (especially the turban variety), cauliflowers, large grapefruits, variegated kale (the leaves can be used separately but should be in water).

Oval
Avocados, lemons, limes, pears, mangoes, artichokes, figs, gourds and aubergines.

Round
Apples (red, yellow, green), oranges, clementines, peppers (red and green), pomegranates, turnips, onions (red and yellow), nectarines, peaches, persimmons, coconuts, artichokes, tangerines, apricots and beets.

Long
Parsnips, carrots, courgettes, aubergines, bananas, cucumbers, gourds, endive, corn-on-the-cob, rhubarb, asparagus, kidney and other beans in long pods.

Clustered (or suitable for clustering)
Grapes, cherries, strawberries, small tomatoes (yellow, red, green), kumquats, garlic, nuts, new potatoes, radishes, Brussels sprouts, small peppers, mushrooms, plums, crab apples, currants (red, white, black), satsumas.

Preparing the fruit

Fruit usually needs a wipe or a wash before use, especially on a dining table where dirt can be seen easily. Wiping with a damp cloth and then buffing with a dry cloth can give a soft sheen to some fruits.

Artificial polish is not suitable and gives a harsh appearance apart from making the fruit inedible.

ORNAMENTAL GARDEN FRUIT

Branches of berries and fruits make beautiful and long-lasting autumn arrangements. They can be arranged alone or combined with flowers and foliage. I cannot decide the reason but I always find arrangements that include branches laden with berries very exciting. It may be the richness of the colours or the sheer opulence of a laden branch. Unfortunately berries have the same attraction for birds and it is often a race to see who gets them first.

To emphasise the lushness of fruit I like long, arching branches arranged traditionally. A centre of interest improves the design and gives density in the middle and for this you can use a few large plain leaves, such as bergenias beginning to turn colour, and either two rosy apples or several chrysanthemums. Hanging clusters of fruits should be clearly seen in space and arranged horizontally so that they can hang down gracefully.

Berries are not often seen successfully arranged in a modern

35 Fruits arranged with candles for a mellow autumn design. The smaller fruits can be secured to the larger ones with cocktail sticks. (*Arranger* Madge Green)

style unless grouped in large bunches, but they do suit drift-wood and landscape styles.

Long life for berries

Berries can last longer than flowers; although a few may drop off, younger ones remain on the stem. The stems are usually woody and should be split and scraped so that they take up water more easily. Some flower arrangers spray berries with hair lacquer or clear varnish. This makes a protective film over the surface and helps to conserve moisture which is lost to the dry atmosphere of a room, in the same way that petals lose moisture. Spraying with water is also helpful.

Some varieties of shrubs to plant

Most berries are found on shrubs and because these tend to be fairly slow-growing the sooner they are planted the better.

Certain varieties are specified in the list below but within some genera there are many types from which to choose and it is worthwhile making an autumn visit to a nursery or garden centre to find those you like. Make sure they are suited to soil and situation.

Arbutus unedo, strawberry tree; a shrub with orange-red globular fruits from October to December. Hardy in the south only.

Acuba japonica, spotted laurel; evergreen shrub with scarlet berries from autumn to spring. Unisexual and needs plants of each sex to berry.

Berberis, deciduous shrubs (those grown for berries); varieties that can have pink-red, yellow, blue or black berries with a waxy bloom. They persist well into winter.

Celastrus orbiculatus; deciduous shrub of climbing habit having pea-sized orange-scarlet fruits, massed on branches, which persist well into winter.

Chaenomeles speciosa, Japanese quince; deciduous shrub bearing medium-sized, round yellow fruits in autumn which are used for preserves.

Cotoneaster; many evergreen and deciduous shrubs with conspicuous berries in autumn, usually scarlet or red, can be cream-yellow.

Crataegus, ornamental thorn; deciduous tree or shrub, red haws.

Euonymus europaea, common spindle tree; deciduous shrub, small rose-red capsules open to show orange seeds.

Hypericum elatum 'Elstead'; semi-evergreen shrub, hardy in south. Large clusters of salmon-red berries in autumn last well in water. *H. calycinum* has black fruits.

Ilex, holly; tree or shrub, with many varieties from which to

36 Berries of cotoneaster, pine-cones and rose hips, with apples on sticks providing emphasis. The container is driftwood screwed to a wooden base with a large food tin screwed to the top to hold water and mechanics — a no-cost, long-term design. (*Arranger* Margaret Stanley)

66

choose including red and yellow berries; male and female plants should be planted together in order to obtain berries, which last on the bushes through winter.

Iris foetidissima; hardy plant with seed pods that split open to reveal scarlet seeds in autumn.

Mahonia X 'Charity'; hardy evergreen shrub with unusual blue berries in clusters, following March and April flowers. I have chosen this hybrid for the excellence of its leaves for arrangements.

Malus, crab apple; deciduous tree or shrub with fruit that can be yellow, red-yellow, crimson-purple, green-yellow or scarlet.

Physalis franchetii, Chinese lantern; a perennial with orange fruits in an orange-red papery calyx that dries well for use in winter arrangements.

Phytolacca americana, poke weed; red-ink plant, perennial with dark purple poisonous berries in October, like blackberries but clustered upright.

Pyracantha, firethorn; evergreen shrubs with many berries, which can be orange-red, yellow or orange-yellow. Unfortunately they are among the birds' favourites.

Rosa moyesii; shrub with flask-shaped red hips 2 inches (5 cm) long in autumn.

Rosa rugosa, 'Frau Dagmar Hastrup'; sturdy shrub with round orange-red hips in early autumn.

Skimmia japonica; evergreen, slow-growing shrub with marvellous scarlet berries but needs male and female plants together and even then can be fickle about berrying.

Sorbus; deciduous trees and shrubs with great quantities of berries in autumn which can be white, yellow, pink, orange or red. *S. aucuparia* is well known as rowan or mountain ash and is often seen in the countryside with large bunches of scarlet berries; it needs defoliating for arrangements as the leaves can look untidy.

Symphoricarpos, snowberry; deciduous shrub bearing large white or pink-white berries well into the new year. Most useful for Christmas arrangements; long-lasting.

Viburnum opulus, guelder rose; deciduous shrub with red, clustered translucent berries in autumn.

Vitis vinifera; a hardy deciduous climber with maroon-coloured grapes and red-purple leaves; sprays with fruit look wonderful with reds.

COUNTRYSIDE FRUITS

Horse chestnuts from the 'conker' tree with shiny brown fruit in prickly cases to use with autumn flowers; leave on branches but remove foliage which is untidy.

Fruit impaled on a toothpick or cocktail stick and inserted into Oasis

Two pieces of fruit joined together

Pineapple held firmly in place on four skewers

Blackberry sprays which look lovely with dahlias and chrysanthemums; remove leaves if poor.

Fir cones can be wired in clusters for autumn and winter arrangements and can be sprayed with metallic paint, glitter or artificial snow for Christmas; also useful for dried plaques.

Larch sprays with small cones can be used as fir cones for Christmas, no wiring necessary; also lovely with small dahlias.

Bulrushes in several heights and diameters add rigid height to an arrangement and can be painted, dyed or glittered; good in water designs in the natural state.

Mountain ash berries; remove leaves and use for autumn, usually hang downwards with weight.

Elderberries which are purple black, but do not last more than a few days. They are attractive with their own foliage as it turns cream, purple and pink, and with bright pink dahlias.

Holly berries, for traditional Christmas designs, are essential.

Ivy berries which are green-black, small and provide 'fillers' in small arrangements. Remove some leaves; long-lasting.

Rose hips, for autumn with small flowers; remove tatty leaves.

Mistletoe; combine with holly and ivy for a traditional Christmas, long-lasting.

Grain stems for small autumn arrangements and dried for winter to use with any smaller flowers; can be sprayed or glittered for Christmas.

Acorns; they need glueing into their cases unless used for plaques.

Iris seed pods which need glycerine treatment to last and turn a brown colour for plaques and smaller dried arrangements, or which can be mixed with fresh flowers.

Wild cherries for clustering by wiring in groups are useful as a change of shape with smaller flowers in autumn.

NUTS

Hard nuts and fruits that dry are invaluable in plaques and three-dimensional pictures. They provide a change of shape and texture. Horse chestnut fruits are a shiny brown. Pecans in their shells are hard, pink and shiny and last indefinitely; they are expensive but worth buying at Christmas when they appear on the market. Walnuts and Brazil nuts in their shells have a rough surface. Hazelnuts are small but a pretty colour.

MECHANICS

Sticks

Fruit rolls around unless carefully placed or anchored. I try not to use wire because it tends to rust and spoil the fruit for eating.

Cocktail sticks and toothpicks do less harm to the fruit. It is easy to impale a fruit on one end of a stick and use the other end to push into mechanics or another piece of fruit. Sometimes greater strength is needed than can be provided by cocktail sticks and wooden (not metal) meat skewers are ideal. If a strong stick of still greater length is needed use a dowel from a do-it-yourself shop. Cut to the desired length and wash it first.

Apples and small oranges can be anchored with cocktail sticks. A pineapple needs as many as four skewers or lengths of dowel pushed into the base to hold it firmly in position. I often begin with one of the bulky fruits such as a melon and then build on other fruits using sticks to hold them in position.

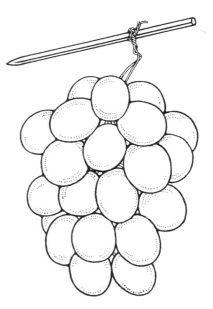

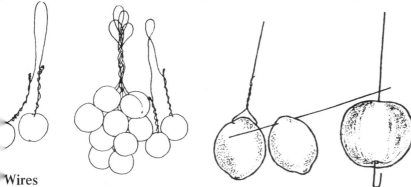

Above Grapes wired on to dowel or skewer
Far left Cherries wired up to form a cluster
Left Wiring a lemon and wiring an apple

Wires

Wire is useful for holding grapes in position. Thread a length of strong wire through the bunch and twist it on to a length of dowel or a skewer; alternatively a thick forked branch is useful.

A cluster of cherries can be made by twisting one end of a lightweight stub wire around one cherry stem and the other around another cherry stem. Continue until you have built up a bunch and then Sellotape the wires together.

If you need to wire other fruits, such as a lemon, make a hole about a quarter of the way down the lemon with a pointed tool such as an ice-pick, then thread through a stub wire and turn up both ends, twisting them around each other to provide a stem.

An alternative way of wiring a strong-tissued fruit such as an apple is to push a stub wire through the centre and turn up a small hook at the bottom to draw up into the base of the fruit.

When wire is inserted through fruit, and not just twisted on to a stem, the fruit is unlikely to be edible later unless the wired part can be successfully cut away.

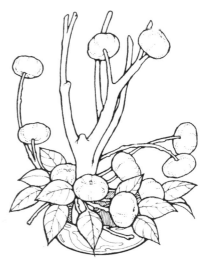

An arrangement of bleached mitsumata and winter camellia with tangerines impaled on the tips of the branches

Fruit on branches

In an arrangement of foliage or flowers, lightweight fruit can be impaled on the tips of strong twigs or branches. The wood should be fresh, not dead, or it will be brittle and snap easily.

37 Roses in a small container of water combined with grapes, red-currants and a little foliage. (*Arranger* Madge Green)

DESIGNING WITH FRUIT

Colour schemes

These depend on your choice of room colourings. If your arrangement is for a dining table you many want to pick up the colours of your china, glasses or tablecloth. Purples, blues and reds are successful together. Greens and yellows are easy to combine; yellows, oranges and reds are harmonious, as are brown, orange and yellow. But a decoration of mixed colours can be equally attractive.

Containers

Flat containers are successful with fruit for there is no need for them to be deep enough to hold water. In fact fruit should not sit in water because it soon becomes mouldy. Cabbages will last a long time out of water. If small numbers of flowers and leaves are used with the fruit, place the stem ends in tubes of water or well-type pinholders concealed amongst the fruit.

Low bowls, flat wooden bases, rush mats, marble slabs, trays of metal or wood, low baskets, cornucopias, elegant epergnes are all suitable. When a deep container is used it is necessary to elevate the fruit with crumpled wire netting or paper. Alternatively upturn a bowl in the centre (held in place with Plasticine) or use a block of dry Oasis.

Kitchen containers such as copper pans are often combined with fruit as an accessory rather than as a container. The fruit can be arranged on a flat base around the utensil.

Composition

Some people say that fruit is difficult to arrange but this is not so if you anchor it firmly. Start in the centre with your largest fruit and build outwards, with transition of size and shape. Round shapes look better in the centre, and then oval, finishing at the extremities with long fruit or clusters such as grapes. These can soften the rim of a container.

A variety of forms is necessary because a grouping of only round fruits looks very static. Two round fruits grouped together are often more pleasing than three of a kind, although more than one group can be used in different positions. There is more unity when, in a group of one kind, stems all face the

38 *Left* A long-lasting autumn fruit arrangement in a Mexican-style container, including sweet corn, chicory, gherkins, red and green peppers, limes, mushrooms, garlic and teasels and pomegranates. It is a fun design with contrasting shapes and textures and gay colouring. (*Arranger* Dorothy Berisford)

39 Autumn fruits and berries including those of cotoneaster, snow-berry, crab apple, ivy, mountain ash and *hypericum*. (*Arranger* Gwen Kirkness)

40 An arrangement of exotic fruits and foliage; the idea could be repeated with more common fruits. The rosettes of echeveria can be left out of water for weeks. (*Arranger* Marian Aaronson)

same way. For example with apples, have either the stems facing front, or the opposite end, but not one of each. When long fruits, such as bananas, are grouped it is more attractive when the tip ends are not level with each other.

Because of its strong forms, fruit can often overwhelm flowers and for this reason it is often combined with bold foliage. However, in the winter months when flowers are scarce two apples can make an excellent centre of interest as a substitute for flowers in an arrangement of evergreens. They can be impaled on sticks pushed into the mechanics in the centre.

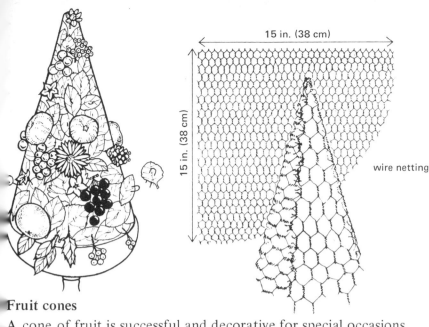

15 in. (38 cm)

15 in. (38 cm)

wire netting

Fruit cones

A cone of fruit is successful and decorative for special occasions and there are several ways of making these. Small fruits can be impaled on sticks and pushed into a dry Oasis cone obtainable from a florist. It is advisable to cover the cone first with glycerined foliage or flat evergreens, using pins or hairpins to hold the leaves in place.

A bigger cone can be made with a triangle of wire netting formed into a cone and filled with dry moss. Impale the fruit on dowels and push them into the moss through the wire netting. Often a mixture of fruit and dried flowers is used for decorations. Any gaps can be filled with long-lived evergreens such as box which lasts well without water.

A cone seen in the decorations in colonial Williamsburg in America was made of wood into which rows of headless nails had been knocked. The fruit was impaled on one or more nails.

A pineapple or larger fruit can be pushed on to the nails on the top and any gaps filled with long-lived evergreens or glycerined foliage. The wooden foundation can stand on a flat base or be elevated on a stemmed container such as a cake plate.

Far left Oasis cone covered first with flat evergreen leaves and glycerined foliage and then decorated with fruits

Above Wire netting cone filled with dry moss and then decorated with dried flowers and fruits

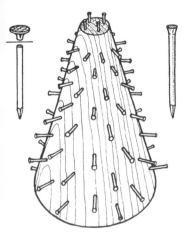

41 *Right* A cone of apples topped with pineapple. The basis is a wooden cone studded with nails to hold the fruit. Long-lasting evergreens fill the gaps. (*Arranger* Dorothy Berisford)

Left Solid wood cone impaled with headless nails

6 WINTER- FLOWERING BULBS

The most welcome of all flowers must surely be the bulb flowers that can be forced for flowering in the depths of winter. They appear at a time when most gardens look dreary and the winter weather is depressing. Cut flowers are expensive and garden flowers almost non-existent from the beginning of the late October frosts, until April brings back the garden flowers. Bulbs supply colour and life in our homes when we need them most. In addition, bulb flowers are easy to grow and last well indoors because they start in bud and gradually unfold their beauty over several weeks for our enjoyment.

It is simply a matter of planning ahead in September. Flowers are inexpensive and plentiful in summer and it is difficult to imagine the stark winter months, but it is well worth while buying bulbs at this time and getting them started. Pots of bulbs also make excellent Christmas gifts and most people cannot have too many. For Christmas flowers bulbs must be bought in September and planted immediately because it takes two or three months for forced bulbs to make a good root system before the leaves and flowers begin to grow.

42 Typically healthy top-quality bulbs (from left to right: daffodil, hyancinth, tulip)

BUYING AND STORING BULBS

Narcissi, large-flowering crocuses, hyacinths, dwarf iris, early double or single tulips and the tiny blue Chionodoxa are the most suitable bulbs for forcing. Look for bulbs marked 'pre-cooled' or 'prepared' or ask the florist or garden centre salesman for bulbs for Christmas or winter flowering. It is important to start with a good bulb, the larger the better, because the flower bud will be formed already inside the bulb at the time of buying. The bulbs for forcing are specially prepared so that they open earlier than normal. They are grown, lifted at the right time, dried carefully and stored at the correct temperature by experts.

The bulbs should feel firm and not have any badly bruised tissue or rot. Daffodil bulbs are graded as single-nosed, double-nosed and mother according to the number of growing points on the bulb (each 'nose' should produce a flower). Rare and newer varieties are expensive and you will be more successful with top-quality bulbs of the more common varieties, which is probably what most florists and garden centres stock anyway.

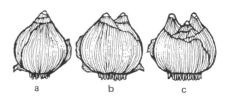

a. Single-nosed daffodil bulb
b. Double-nosed daffodil bulb
c. Mother daffodil bulb

GROWING BULBS IN SOIL

You can plant immediately after buying the bulbs. However, you can have a succession of flowers if you plant a few bulbs each week. Store in a cool, dry, airy place but not for longer than six weeks. A dark place should be used otherwise the bulbs may start shooting like onions, and they should not do this before the root system has grown.

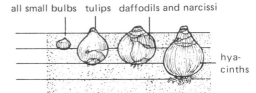

all small bulbs tulips daffodils and narcissi

hya-cinths

Make sure there is enough space in the container for root formation

Containers

Many types of bulb bowl are available or you can use ordinary plant pots, later placing them in outer ornamental pots. They may have drainage holes or not but will need a saucer or an outer pot if they have holes, to avoid drips on the furniture. The container should be at least twice the depth of the bulbs and not less than 5 inches (12cm) deep so that there is space for root growth and watering.

Growing medium

Bulbs will grow in bulb fibre (made up especially for the purpose), in John Innes No. 2 compost, or in water in some cases (see page 79). It is advisable to use packets of fibre or compost sold in garden centres because this is sterilised and free of bugs, bacteria and fungus. The advantage of using John Innes No. 2 is that the flowers should appear again the following year when planted in the garden. Bulbs planted in fibre have no food and take two years to flower in the garden but the fibre is very clean to handle. Bulb fibre is the most suitable medium for pots without holes because it remains sweet throughout the growing season.

43 Crocus growing in bulb fibre

44 A full bowl of bulb flowers looks better than a sparsely-filled one

a. Put a layer of crocks or pebbles in the bottom of a clay pot (peat if you are using a plastic pot)
b. Put a layer of compost or special bulb fibre and press down
c. Arrange the bulbs shoulder to shoulder, pointed end upwards, pressing down firmly but not screwing them in.
d. Add more compost or fibre so that only the bulb tips show

Bulbs grown in water will possibly never flower again. No forced bulbs will be any use in the house again and should be planted out-of-doors after flowering.

No feeding of bulbs is necessary because the flowers are already formed inside the bulb.

Bulbs need
1 A period in a dark cool place for root formation.
2 A shorter time in a shady cool place for acclimatising.
3 Later warmth and light for flower formation.

Method of planting in fibre or compost

You will need

Bulbs

Container. When clay pots are used soak them in water overnight because otherwise they will absorb moisture from the compost.

Bulb fibre or John Innes No. 2, soaked overnight and then squeezed out.

Pebbles or crocks (for pots without holes)

Method

Some people find bulbs irritate the skin and you may wish to wear gardening gloves when planting. Certainly wash your hands well immediately afterwards.

1 Place a layer of pebbles or crocks in the bottom of the pot to provide drainage if there is no hole.

2 Add a layer of compost or bulb fibre and press it down gently.

3 Nestle the bulbs into the fibre or compost arranging them so that they almost touch each other, pointed end upwards. If a bulb has a lot of dry roots at the bottom, cut them off. A full bowl of flowers looks much better than a sparsely filled one. If you plant all the same variety of bulb in one pot the flowers will appear at the same time and this looks more attractive.

a   b   c   d

4 Add more fibre or compost so that the tips of the bulbs are showing if they are large bulbs. Smaller bulbs should be covered with half an inch (1cm) of compost. Be certain to leave at least half an inch (1cm) of space between the top of the compost and the rim of the container so that the bulbs can be watered without spillage.

5 Water after planting if the compost seems dry.

6 It is a good idea to label each pot with the contents because it is easy to forget what you have planted during the following weeks.

Double potting

A mass of colour can be obtained by planting daffodils in a double layer. Two layers each of three bulbs can be planted in a 6 inch (15cm) pot. 'Golden Harvest' and 'King Alfred' are good varieties to use. Narcissi can be similarly planted and paper-white 'Grandiflora' and 'Geranium' are suitable.

Below left Double planting daffodil or narcissi bulbs

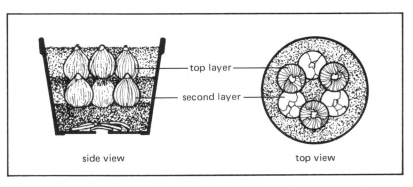

top layer — second layer —

side view   top view

Put a 2 inch (5cm) layer of moist bulb fibre in the bottom of the pot and press in three bulbs, equidistant from each other. Cover the bulbs to their necks with more fibre and then press in three more bulbs between the necks of the first bulbs. Again cover these with fibre, packing it firmly around the bulbs to within 1 inch (2.5cm) of the top of the pot, to allow for watering.

Place in the dark, as described below, for about ten weeks and then continue the normal process of acclimatisation. The bulbs can be planted in the garden later.

Root formation

Good root growth must be encouraged before leaves and flowers appear, and to enable this to happen it is necessary to store the bowls in a cool, dark place such as a dry cellar or attic, a cupboard, a shelf in a coalhouse or a garden shed. If a dark place is not available you can keep the bulbs in the dark by placing over them an inverted plant pot (with the hole in the top blocked or covered) or a box, or a brown paper bag.

Bulbs can also be plunged in the garden and many gardeners prefer to do this, although I find it easier to check the moisture

a

b   c

Above a. Store the planted bulbs in a cool, dark place like a cupboard or cellar. b. The pots can be left outside in a moderately cold climate in boxes packed with straw, wood shavings, ash or moist peat to prevent freezing. c. If you have no dark storage place cover the bulbs with an inverted plant pot, first blocking up the drainage hole

77

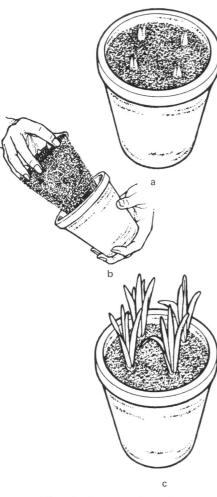

and growth if they are indoors. Plunge them in a trench or a box, out of warm sunny positions and cover them with straw, wood shavings, ash or moist peat to a depth of about 6 inches (15cm). They should not be allowed to freeze.

Check the bulbs about every three weeks for dryness and water if necessary but the compost should never be waterlogged.

Moving the pots into the light

When the tips of the leaves are pale green points above the surface of the compost (about 2 inches (5cm), of growth should be showing) the pots can be taken out of the dark.

Another more daring method of checking that the bulbs are ready for the next stage is to turn the pot upside down, tap its side gently allowing the compost and bulbs to slide into your hand. Roots should be visible at the bottom or the edge of the compost before bringing the pot into the light, otherwise return bulbs and compost to the pot. Normally the pots can be taken out of the dark about eight to twelve weeks after planting but this varies with different bulbs. A delay of four or five weeks will do no harm even if the bulbs show the necessary leaf development. If delayed you can then have a succession of flowers.

Sudden heat is not advisable after the pot is first placed in the light and a window ledge or porch where it is cool is suitable at first. When the leaves are opening up and about 4 inches (10cm) high the bowls can be removed to a warmer position to encourage the flower buds. For all plants and cut flowers hot or draughty positions should be avoided; these include over an open fire, radiator or television set. A sunny window does not matter in winter because the sun is not strong enough to do much harm.

Water the compost when dry and turn the bowl sometimes so that light falls evenly on the bulbs and they develop at the same time.

STAKING

Lengthy stems and heavy flower heads need support and small sticks can be bought for this purpose at garden centres or do-it-yourself shops. Push a stick into the compost near each bulb, being careful not to pierce the bulb. Then use garden string or yarn to tie each stem to its stick in one or more places. Another method is to weave the string around the sticks and stems but this can look unattractive.

Aftercare

Remove dead flowers as they fade, but not the leaves or stems because these feed the bulbs for another year if you are going to plant them in the garden.

When all the flowers have faded move the bowl to a cool,

a. The plants are ready to be moved into a cool, light place (sunny window ledge or conservatory) when the tips of the leaves show pale green above the surface
b. Check root formation by removing compost and bulbs gently and examining the root ball.
c. Move the plants to a warmer place when the leaves are beginning to open up and are about 4 inches (10cm) high

ight place and keep the bulbs watered, decreasing the water as the foliage begins to yellow. Then lift the bulbs in March or April and plant them in the garden, compost and bulbs together. If you are going to discard them after flowering it does not matter about removing the leaves and stems.

GROWING IN WATER

Hyacinth and tazetta narcissi are the most suitable bulbs for growing in water. Special forcing glasses are made and you can watch the roots growing, which is fascinating to children, although decoratively I do not find these glasses as attractive as bulb bowls.

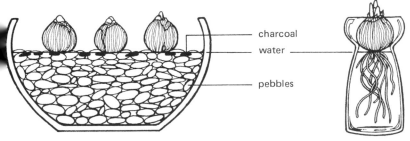

charcoal
water
pebbles

Growing bulbs in water in a bowl or a special bulb jar

The bulb should just touch the water; later only the roots should be submerged. A few pieces of charcoal keep the water sweet and tap water can be used. Forcing glasses hold only one bulb but you can use water and pebbles in a larger bowl. The pebbles support the bulbs with water below. Again, the bulbs should not sit deeply in the water.

To encourage the roots to grow place the containers of water and bulbs in a cool position until the shoots on the top are about 1 inch (2.5cm) high and the roots 3-4 inches (8-10cm) long. Hyacinth should be kept in the dark during the time of root formation but tazetta narcissi can be stood on a window sill. Then gradually bring into full light and finally warmth, adding water when necessary. The bulbs are normally discarded after flowering as they will not flower again because their roots have been adapted to water and not soil.

DECORATIVE USE OF BULB FLOWERS

It is a good idea to plant up some single bulbs in pots. These can be used to push into a bowl of mixed plants to add colour. They will grow on as they do in their own pots.

Groups of pots of bulbs look better than single pots, in the same way that a group of plants becomes a feature in a room. Tall growing flowers such as narcissi can be placed at the back and shorter-stemmed flowers in the front.

The compost at the base of a bowl of bulbs can look bare. Using a large bulb bowl you can push a small plant into the centre of the compost at the time of planting the bulbs. Then

45 A decorative arrangement can be made with hyacinths at the back and horizontal plants which cover the bare foreground

when the bowl of bulbs is moved indoors a small spreading plant can be inserted in place of the plant pot.

CHOOSING YOUR BULBS

Indoor hyacinths

Buy bulbs at least 7 inches (17cm) in circumference.
Plant in bowls at least 5 inches (13cm) deep.
Leave 8-15 weeks in a cool dark place, depending on the variety
Start planting at the beginning of October, at two-week intervals, for 6-8 weeks.
They flower 3-4 weeks after being acclimatised.
Those listed under 'early-flowering' may be brought into the home during January, later-flowering bulbs should be brought indoors in mid to late February.

Note
The following lists of bulbs give a month at the end of each description. This is the time when the bulbs can be brought indoors from the plunge and forced into flower.

Early flowering hyacinths

Colour	Name	Description	Time of flowering
White	'Blizzard'	pure white, large solid spike	mid-January
	'L'Innocence'	pure white, loosely set bells	end January
Yellow	'Yellow Hammer'	creamy yellow, short sturdy spike	end January
Orange	'Orange Boven'	apricot-salmon, compact truss	end January
Pink	'Anne Marie also known as 'Ann Mary'	bright salmon-pink, neat head	early January
	'Lady Derby'	shell-pink, large bells	end January
	'La Victoire'	carmine-pink, strong spike	mid-January
	'Pink Pearl'	clear pink, broad spike	mid-January
	'Princess Irene'	silvery rose-pink, large spike	end January
Red	'Jan Bos'	crimson-red, strong spike	early January
	'Madame du Barry'	crimson-scarlet	mid-January
Blue	'Bismark'	porcelain-blue	end January
	'Blue Giant'	mid-blue	end January

Colour	Name	Description	Time of flowering
Blue (continued)	'Delft Blue'	shining porcelain-blue, fine form	mid-January
	'Marie'	dark blue	mid-January
	'Myosotis'	light sky-blue, fine form	end January
	'Ostara'	navy blue, magnificent spike	mid-January
	'Perle Brilliante'	pale ice-blue, large bells	end January
Mauve	'Lord Balfour'	mauve-violet, large bells	end January

Late-flowering hyacinths

Colour	Name	Description	Time of flowering
White	'Carnegie'	pure white, large broad spike	mid-February
Yellow	'City of Harlem'	creamy lemon-white, large truss	mid-February
Pink	'Crown Princess'	soft ice-pink, large truss	early February
	'Margaretha'		
	'Queen of the Pinks'	bright rose-pink, compact spike	mid-February
Blue	'Blue Jacket'	dark blue, magnificent spike	early February
	'King of the Blues'	indigo-blue, compact spike	mid-February
	'Queen of the Blues'	pastel blue, large spike	mid-February
Mauve	'Amethyst'	lilac-mauve, abundant flowers	mid-February
Red	'Amsterdam'	cerise red, sturdy reddish stem	mid-February

Christmas-flowering varieties

These must be specially prepared and planted in early September.

Colour	Name	Description	Time of flowering
White	'Carnegie'	pure white, large broad spike	late December
	'Colosseum'	white	late December
	'L'Innocence'	pure white, loosely set bells	late December

Colour	Name	Description	Time of flowering
Blue	'Blue Giant'	mid-blue	late December
	'Delft Blue'	shining, porcelain-blue, fine form	late December
	'Ostara'	navy blue, magnificent spike	late December
Yellow	'Yellow Hammer'	creamy yellow, short sturdy spike	late December
Pink	'Anna Marie'	bright salmon-pink, neat head	late December
	'Lady Derby'	shell-pink, large bells	late December
	'Pink Pearl'	clear pink, broad spike	late December
	'Rosalie'	light pink, slightly smaller than standard	late December
Red	'Amsterdam'	cerise-red, study reddish stem	late December
	'Jan Bos'	crimson-red, strong spike	late December

Indoor tulips

Plant 8-10 in a 6 inch (15cm) diameter pot.

Start in early September, planting until mid-October.

Leave 10-12 weeks in a cool, dark position.

Then place in a dark but slightly warmer position for 2-3 weeks, maximum 60°F (16°C).

When they have grown a further 1-2 inches (2.5-5cm), move to a lighter room.

They should be brought indoors from mid-January (those planted in early September for Christmas flowering should be brought in by 1 December).

Single early tulips

Name	Colour	Height	Time of flowering	Comments
'Bellona'	golden-yellow	15in. (38cm)	last two weeks of January	easy to force
'Brilliant Star'	scarlet	12in. (30cm)	from mid-January	easy to force
'Dr Plesman'	orange-red	14in. (35cm)	last two weeks of Janaury	
'Pink Beauty'	pink and white	13in. (33cm)	second week of February	
'Keizerskroon'	red and yellow	13in. (33cm)	last two weeks of Janaury	

Double early tulips

Name	Colour	Height	Time of flowering	Comments
'Electra'	cherry-red	11in. (28cm)	second week of February	
'Marechal Niel'	yellow and orange	11in. (28cm)	second week of February	
'Mr van der Hoef'	golden-yellow	11in. (28cm)	second week of February	
'Orange Nassau'	orange-scarlet	11in. (28cm)	second week of February	
'Peach Blossom'	rosy-pink	11in. (28cm)	second week of February	

Mendel tulips

Name	Colour	Height	Time of flowering	Comments
'Apricot Beauty'	salmon, tinged red	16in. (40cm)	for forcing from late January	easy to force
'Athleet'	pure white	18in. (45cm)	for forcing from late January	
'Krelage's Triumph'	crimson-red	24in. (60cm)	for forcing from late January	
'Olga'	violet-red	18in. (45cm)	for forcing from late January	
'Pink Trophy'	Pink, flushed rose	20in. (50cm)	for forcing from late Janaury	
'Sulphur Triumph'	primrose-yellow	22in. (56cm)	for forcing from late January	
'Van der Ederen'	glowing red	19in. (48cm)	for forcing from late January	

Triumph tulips

Name	Colour	Height	Time of flowering	Comments
'Crater'	carmine-red	18in. (45cm)	for forcing from mid-February	
'Edith Eddy'	carmine-red, edged white	20in. (50cm)	for forcing from mid-February	
'Garden Party'	white, edged carmine	16in. (40cm)	for forcing from mid-February	easy to force
'Keen Nelis'	blood-red, edged yellow	20in. (50cm)	for forcing from mid-February	easy to force
'K&M's Triumph'	vermilion, tinged carmine	25in. (63cm)	for forcing from mid-February	
'Princess Beatrix'	orange-scarlet, edged yellow	24in. (60cm)	for forcing from mid-February	
'Prominence'	dark red	21in. (53cm)	for forcing from mid-February	
'Reforma'	sulphur-yellow	18in. (45cm)	for forcing from mid-February	
'Topscore'	geranium-red	24in. (60cm)	from mid-January	

Darwin Hybrid tulips

Name	Colour	Height	Time of flowering	Comments
'Apeldoorn'	orange-scarlet	24in. (60cm)	for forcing from late January	
'Beauty of Apeldoorn'	yellow, flushed magenta	24in. (60cm)	for forcing from late January	
'Dover'	poppy-red	26in. (66cm)	for forcing from late January	
'Gudoshnik'	sulphur-yellow, tinted red	26in. (66cm)	for forcing from late January	
'Jewel of Spring'	sulphur-yellow, edged red	26in. (66cm)	for forcing from late January	

Lily-flowered tulips

Name	Colour	Height	Time of flowering	Comments
'Aladdin'	scarlet, edged yellow	20in. (50cm)	for forcing from mid-February	
'Mariette'	deep satin-rose	24in. (60cm)	for forcing from mid February	
'White Triumphator'	pure white	26in. (66cm)	for forcing from mid-February	

Christmas-flowering varieties

Name	Colour	Height	Time of flowering	Comments
'Brilliant Star'	bright scarlet	12in. (30cm)	late December	
'Brilliant Star Maximus'	post office red	12in. (30cm)	late December	
'Christmas Marvel'	cherry-pink	14in. (35cm)	late December	
'Joffre'	yellow	10in. (25cm)	late December	easy to force

Indoor daffodils

Plant from early September and allow 12-16 weeks for root formation.

When brought indoors to acclimatise keep the temperature at about 50°F (10°C), otherwise they will grow too tall.

When flower buds are visible move to a warmer position. Spray water lightly over the buds just before they open.

Remove the foliage of sideshoots if these do not show a flower bud.

Cooler conditions mean that the flowers will last longer.

Types recommended for indoor forcing include:

Trumpets

Name	Colour	Time of flowering
'Beersheba'	pure white	from late February
'Celebrity'	white and primrose	from late February
'Explorer'	yellow	from early February
'Goblet'	white and yellow	from early February
'Golden Harvest'	golden-yellow	from early February
'King Alfred'	deep yellow	from early February
'Magnificence'	rich yellow	from early February
'Mount Hood'	pure white	from late February
'Rembrandt'	mimosa yellow	from late February
'Unsurpassable'	buttercup-yellow	from late February
'W.P. Milner'	mimosa-yellow turning cream (miniature)	from late February

Large cupped

Name	Colour	Time of flowering
'Brunswick'	white and lime yellow	from early February
'Carlton'	soft yellow	from early February
'Delibes'	yellow and golden orange	from late February
'Flower Record'	white and golden-yellow	from late February
'Fortune'	yellow and orange	from early February
'Mrs R.O. Backhouse'	white and pink	from early February
'Scarlet Elegance'	yellow and orange-red	from late February

Type	Name	Colour	Time of flowering
Small-cupped	'Barrett Browning'	white and flame	from early February
	'Edward Buxton'	primrose and yellow-orange	from late February
	'La Riante'	white and orange-red	from late February
Double	'Cheerfulness'	white and yellow	from late February
	'Irene Copeland'	creamy-white and apricot	from late February
	'Texas'	cream, gold and tangerine	from early February
	'Yellow Cheer-fulness'	golden-yellow	from late February
Cyclami-neus	'February Gold'	deep golden-yellow	from early February
	'March Sunshine'	deep gold	from early February
	'Peeping Tom'	golden-yellow	from early February
Poeticus	'Actea'	white, yellow and red	from late February

Christmas-flowering varieties (specially prepared)

Type	Name	Colour	Time of flowering
Trumpets	'Poetaz Cragford'	milk-white with orange-scarlet cup	late December
	'Golden Harvest'	golden-yellow	late December
Large-cupped	'Patriarch'	white with tangerine-apricot cup	late December
	'Smiling Queen'	white with golden-orange cup	late December
	'Valiant Spark'	yellow with tangerine-orange cup	late December
	'Yellow Sun'	yellow with golden-yellow cup	late December
Small-cupped	'Verger'	white with lemon-yellow cup, bordered orange	late December
Double	'Texas'	cream, gold and tangerine	late December
Cyclami-neus	'Peeping Tom'	rich golden-yellow trumpet	late December

7 DRIED FLOWER DECORATIONS

46 A large traditional arrangement can be made of dried plant material and remain in position for many weeks. This pedestal design includes glycerined beech, eucalyptus, sea grape leaves, rhododendron, dried palm leaves, dried flowers of hydrangea, protea and achillea, seedheads of poppy, hollyhock and acanthus with gourds in shades of brown, blue and yellow. (*Arranger* Dorothy Berisford)

If you have a few stems of dried flowers, you can always make an arrangement that is long lasting. Dried flowers are easy to find these days. They have become popular because of central heating and can be bought in shops and garden centres, gleaned from the countryside and grown in the garden. Many restaurants, hotels and shops would go undecorated without dried arrangements because of central heating, the expense of flowers and the lack of personnel to arrange them.

There is a use for dried plant material in every home. You can make a large or a small design entirely with dried flowers and they can be arranged in modern as well as traditional styles, according to the setting. If you still prefer fresh flowers, you can combine fresh and dried plant material. This means that you need not buy so many fresh flowers because the dried ones can extend them into a bigger arrangement. I find this the most important use for dried flowers in my home.

Dried flowers can be almost indestructible, but their long life can also be a drawback because they are sometimes left so long in an arrangement that they become dusty, damaged and untidy. It is essential to give the flowers occasional attention, either to renew the plant material or to freshen it up and rearrange it.

There is greater scope in design when using dried and preserved plant material because you are not hampered by the transient quality of fresh flowers. Dried plant material is less fragile and you can work on a design for longer and without the anxiety of damaging the flowers. It is possible to bend, twist and cut many dried materials to create new forms and, because they need no water, positions in the design can be varied and unconventional. For this reason dried plant material is often used in modern and abstract designs. Many dried materials, such as driftwood and seedheads, have strong forms and a sculptural beauty that especially suits modern styles.

In addition to making flower arrangements with dried plant material, you can also make plaques, pictures and swags for hanging on a wall, and calendars and greetings cards to send away to friends. Christmas decorations can be made using dried plant material that has been glittered and sprayed with metallic paint. Small decorations can be made for gift parcels and boxes, and paper-weights can be embedded with dried flowers. New decorative uses for dried plant material are constantly being discovered.

THE DIFFERENCE BETWEEN 'DRIED' AND 'PRESERVED'

There are two methods of making flowers and leaves last beyond their normal life span. One is to remove the water content, leaving behind the skeleton as 'dried' plant material. The other method is to replace the water with glycerine, the result being described as 'preserved'. Not all plant material is suitable for both methods and some is unsuitable for either. But there is still plenty of choice. Leaves are generally preserved because few dry successfully, and flowers are usually dried because few preserve well.

THE COLOURS

There is a tendency to think of dried and preserved arrangements as brown in colour, and for this reason some people dislike them for being 'colourless' as well as lifeless. Preserved plant material is usually brown, but in many shades from light cream to almost black. However, there are many other lovely colours in dried plant material including blues and mauves, reds and pinks, greens, yellows and oranges. The colours are less brilliant than those of fresh flowers but they are still attractive. Some dried plant material is dyed and although subtle artificial colours are to be found there are many that are garish.

SOURCES OF SUPPLY

You can either buy dried and preserved plant material or treat fresh material yourself.

Shops and garden centres

There is now an enormous variety of dried plant material from which to make a choice. There are bunches of one variety of flower or leaf, mixed packets, or single leaves, flowers or seedheads. It is a matter of deciding what you like and what suits the intended setting of the decoration.

Supplies come from all over the world and enterprising buyers import exotic specimens as well as stocking the more commonplace. Plant material from tropical and sub-tropical countries is often interesting, bold in form and seemingly indestructible. Those from temperate zones are plentiful and varied.

Gardens and countryside

It is easy enough to collect your own dried material at no cost. There is much of the squirrel's hoarding nature in many of us and we delight in harvesting nature's bounty whether it be as jams and preserves or dried plant material for decorative use.

In addition to collecting naturally dried materials you can grow your own fresh flowers and leaves to dry and preserve. Many seedsmen now offer special collections for this purpose (see page 141 for list of address). A little work during summer and early autumn can result in masses of gleanings at little or no cost.

DRYING PLANT MATERIAL

Success with drying is easy. It is a matter of choosing suitable plant material and then using the correct method to dry it. When a plant reaches the end of its growth cycle it gradually stops taking up water and eventually shrivels and dies. The techniques of drying concern the removal of water with a minimum of shrivelling so that the form remains attractive.

There are several drying methods and each will be described in turn: natural drying, hanging up in warm air, standing in shallow water, drying in high temperature, burying in a desiccant, and pressing (see Chapter 9).

Natural drying

Plants respond differently as they dry out. Although some shrivel, others keep their shape because of their rigid structure. They can be seen standing upright without trace of shrivelling in the garden or countryside throughout the autumn and often in the winter. You can cut them over a period of many weeks and they need no further treatment. It is advisable not to leave cutting them until late autumn because of weather damage. They can be used at once in arrangements.

Hanging up in warm air

Some flowers will dry naturally but shrivel or disintegrate quickly, hang their heads in the process, or easily become weather-damaged unless prevented. The majority of flowers (exceptions are hydrangeas and achilleas and other flowers that dry standing in water), are better cut and brought indoors just before they reach maturity because they continue to mature after being cut. Quick drying indoors helps to prevent shrivelling and gives better colour retention. Any dry, preferably warm, place is suitable, such as an airing cupboard, spare bedroom or boiler room.

It is better to hang the flowers upside down because this keeps the top of the stem rigid as it dries; some plants such as bells-of-Ireland and *Acanthus* hang their heads when dried upright. They can be tied to a washing line, if you have a place

A clothes rack makes a good drying frame for plant material

to rig it up, to coat hangers or to a portable or fixed clothes drying rack.

Drying in the dark is thought to help colour retention, but a dark place is not always available. Small bunches and single flowers can be tied in brown paper bags. Never use polythene bags for the drying process because these hold in the moisure that you want to remove and the plant material becomes mouldy.

Preparation of stems

Cut on a dry day if you can because there will be less water to remove from the flower. Cut the stem as long as possible and remove the leaves (these delay dehydration and are of no decorative use because they shrivel).

The larger specimens, such as huge delphiniums, should be hung singly as they might be crushed when hung in a bunch. Other flowers can be tied in small bunches but with the flowers separated so that they do not squash each other. They will all dry out in a few days and should feel crisp and papery to the touch.

Standing in water

Some plants are better dried gradually while standing in water (an inch of water is normally sufficient). Heathers, proteas and achilleas suit this method. This also applies to hydrangeas which take a long time to dry out completely; some parts still need water while others are already dry. The flowers can be used in an arrangement while they dry.

Drying in high temperature

Some plant material dries when placed in hot air. This is a good method for artichokes and fruits such as gourds, avocados,

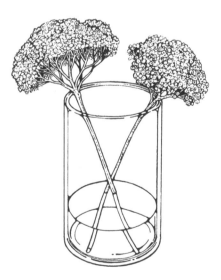

Heather, proteas and achilleas dry gradually while standing in a little water

Tie coloured ribbon round the orange and stud each quarter with even rows of cloves, using a cocktail stick or toothpick to pierce the holes. Roll the finished pomander in spices

Tying pliable stems round a lampshade ring and drying for a few days will prodice twirling stems

pomegranates and fungi. Choose fruits that are unblemished and not quite ripe. Place them on a wire cake rack in a dark corner of a hot airing cupboard, or near a boiler, and let them dry out gradually. They take time, which varies according to the amount of water in the fruit, the heat of the cupboard and the fruit size. Large gourds could take three months. So forget about them for a while. Eventually they will feel hard and lightweight. You may find that some have become mouldy, but this can be discouraged by wiping them with a mild disinfectant before placing them in the hot air.

Small oranges can be studded with cloves, which are a preservative, and dried in this way to provide sweet-smelling pomanders to hang amongst your clothes.

Pliable stems such as those of broom can be soaked for 24 hours and then tied around a lampshade ring and dried in hot air. After a few days they can be untied and you will have twirling stems.

Storage of dried plant material

Dried plant material must always be stored in a dry place or it can re-absorb water and become mouldy. Dried flowers can be left hanging where you placed them, but you may prefer to pack them away, and certainly colour retention is better if they are stored away from strong light.

Some flowers such as delphiniums tend to be rather fragile and to crush easily and it is worth packing precious specimens carefully. Large flower boxes with tissue paper to support the heads are advisable. Cover the open boxes with stretched clingfilm and replace the lids. You will then be able to see what is in each box without disturbance and the film also excludes moisture. Tougher plant material such as straw flowers can remain in bunches stored in boxes and any with rigid structures such as achilleas and poppy seedheads can be stood in wide jars. I find this a good storage method because I can find what I want quickly.

True 'everlastings'

There are some annual flowers that may be kept for years without any change of appearance and which dry naturally on the plants. See page 141 for list of seed merchants.

Cultivation

Follow instructions on the seed packets or sow under glass in late March (many do not need glass). Prick out seedlings and grow on in cold frames until gradually hardened off prior to planting out at the beginning of June.

Harvesting

Harvesting will vary in different climates and will be earlier in the south than in the north. The end of July to the beginning of September is a general guide.

Name	Description	Variety	Comments
Ammobium alatum	flowers up to 1in. (2.5cm) across, bright and glistening with silvery white petals, yellow centres on 18-24in (45-60cm) stems	'Grandiflorum'	
Amaranthus caudatus	drooping, long flowers		cut when very young
Amaranthus paniculatus	(like tails) in green and red, 6in. (15cm) and longer, 2ft (60cm) high	'Green Feathers' 'Green Necklace', 'Viridis'	
Gomphrena globosa	oval flower heads 1-1½in. (2.5-3cm) long on 5-6in. (12-15cm) stems	'Goldie', 'Buddy', 'Royal Purple', Mixed	
Helichrysum bracteatum	everlasting or strawflower, up to 2in. (5cm) across, many-petalled, opening to show a dominant yellow or gold centre, feels papery. Dwarf are 12in. (30cm) in height		
Helipterum humboldtianum	daisy-like, straw-textured flowers in clusters, yellow but turn green after drying, 15in. (40cm) stems		
Helipterum manglesii	single red or white, daisy like flowers up to 1½ in. (4.5cm) across with a yellow centre; slightly drooping sometimes, 15in. (40cm) stems	Alba, Alba pura, Maculata rosea, Mixed	
Helipterum roseum	semi-double, rose-coloured or white flowers, 1in. (2.5cm) across, 15in (40cm) stems		cut in bud
Helipterum grandiflorum	white with black centre, with yellow centre, pink with yellow centre, pink with black centre, red with yellow centre, red with black centre, mixed		
Limonium sinuatum (Statice sinuata)	broadly winged stems with 3-4in. (7.5-10cm) long clusters of flowers with green bracts	Rainbow mixture, White, Market Growers blue, 'Lavender Queen',	

Name	Description	Variety	Comments
Limonium sinuatum (continued)		Rosea Superba, Easy Grow Deep Night, 'Chigasaki Murasaki'	
Linonium suworowii	rose pink flowers densely packed in narrow plume-like panicles up to 18in. (45cm) long		
Lonas annua (L. inodora)	tight clusters of small ball-shaped golden-yellow flowers, 12in. (30cm) in height		
Xeranthemum annuum	daisy-like, papery-petalled, 24in. (60cm) stems	Mixed double varieties	

Grasses

These include wild grasses that are picked when young and ornamentals that can be bought separately or in mixed packet from the seed houses listed (see page 141).

Cultivation

Sow under glass (unless otherwise stated), a few seeds to a pot in late March, and do not thin, to minimise disturbance. After hardening off, plant out in early to mid-May, according to late spring frosts.

Harvesting

Cut grasses between the end of June and the beginning of September according to your part of the country. Hang up to dry; it is worth experimenting with glycerine treatment for a few of each that you grow to see if the results differ.

Name	Height	Description
Briza maxima (quaking grass)	18in. (45cm)	large spikes of green and white
Polypogon monspeliensis	18in. (45cm)	panicle spike-like
Festuca incrassata	12in. (30cm)	blue-tufted grass
Lagurus ovatus	24in. (60cm)	hare's tail grass. Soft woolly plumes up to 2in. (5cm) carried singly on long stems up to 24in. (60cm) in height
Bromus madritensis, B. lanceolatus, B. secalinus, B. unioloides	18in. (45cm)	spikelets on stems up to 18in. (45cm) high

Name	Height	Description
Pennisetum	24in. (60cm)	bottlebrush-like flower heads in off-white, sometimes purple, on stems up to 24in. (60cm) in height
Triticum spelta, T. durum	24in. (60cm)	wheat-like spike
Helictotrichon sempervirens (Syn. Avena candida)	48in. (20cm)	oat-like spikelets on long stems
Hordeum jubatum	18in. (45cm)	squirrel-tail grass, silky, long-haired barley-like tassels, silver-grey, 18in. (45cm) in height
Coix lacryma-jobi	24in. (60cm)	(Job's tears). Pendulous clusters of grey-green woody seeds on stems up to 24in. (60cm) high
Phalaris canariensis	18in. (45cm)	canary grass. Oval-shaped spikes
Setaria italica, S. viridis, S. 'Nandi'	18-24in. (45-60cm)	a form of foxtail millet with large, nodding gold heads, when dry up to 5in. (12.5cm) long

Seedheads

Name	Description	Colour	Comments
Alliums – Allium giganteum, A. aflatunense, A. moly, A. cepa (onion), A. porrum (leek), A Albopilosum	in a number of sizes, spherical heads	mauve to beige	
Angelica archangel-ica	perennial, large, rough-textured spheres	green to beige	
Papaver somniferum	annual poppies — medium cylinders with a cap	beige	
Aruncus sylvester	goat's beard, perennial	beige spikes	
Typha latifolia	bulrushes (great reedmace) velvety cylinders (wild)	dark brown	
Anthriscus sylvestris	cow parsley (wild) dainty, fragile	cream	
Dipsacus follonum	teasel, biennial, prickly, cylindrical	beige	

Name	Description	Colour	Comments
Rumex longifolius	dock (wild) up to 36in. (90cm), rough texture	rich brown	
Lunaria annua	honesty, biennial, small papery	silver discs	
Nigella	love-in-a-mist, annual, inflated seed-pod, 1in. (2.5cm) long	pale brown	
Helianthus annus	sunflowers, annual, large seedheads	dark brown	good for modern arrangement

Plants suitable for air-drying
Easy to grow and dry
The time taken depends on the size and water content of the flowers and the dryness of the room in which the flowers are hung.

Name	Description	Comments
Acanthus mollis	bear's breeches, perennial, bold spikes	pick when florets open right up the stem
Alchemilla mollis	lady's mantle, perennial, dainty branched heads of tiny star-like flowers	
Amaranthus caudatus	love-lies-bleeding, half-hardy annuals, drooping tassels	
Anaphalis	pearly everlasting, perennial	pick before flowers have begun to fluff
Physalis	chinese lanterns	cut in September
Cynara cardunculus	cardoons, perennial, large thistle-like heads	pick in full flower
Cynara scolymus	globe artichokes, perennial, large thistle-like heads	pick in full flower
Delphinium	perennial, tall spikes	three days in airing cupboard in full flower
Echinops ritro	perennial, spiky spherical heads, blue	pick before maturity
Eryngium	sea hollies, perennial, teasel-like heads with metallic sheen	
Larkspur	annual, branched spikes	treat as delphiniums
Lavender	perennial, fragrant spikes	
Lonas	annual, clusters of small ball-shaped flowers	

Burying in a desiccant

Desiccants are substances that can absorb and retain 50 per cent of their own weight in water from plants that have been buried in them to dry. This method is used for flowers such as roses with many petals that cannot be dried by other methods. But the results are fragile and are suitable only for people prepared to take care and patience in handling and storage. They are not practical for normal use.

Desiccants

Suitable desiccants are sand, borax, alum, silica gel, yellow cornmeal, or a mixture of any of these. All have a different grain and weight; small grains are better for very thin-tissued fragile flowers such as single roses and larger, heavier grains for coarser flowers such as dahlias. It is a matter of finding a good balance; the flower petals need the support of the grains but should not be crushed by them.

Sand has been used for generations but is heavy. Alum and borax are very light because they are fine-grained, but they are inclined to stick in the crevices of petals. Most people now buy commercial products that are well advertised. Normally these are silica gel ground down to a useful grain size and weight. It is possible to buy two different powders for different types of flowers. Silica gel from a chemist is usually sold in large granules which are too heavy unless hammered down with a rolling pin. The commercial products can seem expensive at the time of buying but give reliable results and can be used over and over again. Through experience flower arrangers decide their own preference for a desiccant. Many people make their own compounds after experiments using different flowers and desiccants.

Time taken to dry

In addition to using the correct grain the time taken to dry flowers is important and affects the results; too long and the flowers become brittle, too short and they will not be fully dry and the petals will collapse. Again it is a matter of experiment. Generally sand is the slowest, taking two to three weeks in room temperature; silica gel is the fastest, taking two to three days. Alum and borax take seven to ten days.

Flower arrangers have discovered that desiccants work more rapidly in a warm place and some people, wishing for quick results, place the container of desiccant in which the flower is buried in a warm oven. Others achieve good results using a microwave oven. No metal should be used in this case, so omit any wire stems and place the desiccant in anything but a metal container. Place in the oven for about two and a half minutes for a small rose such as the variety 'Carol'. It is little trouble to experiment with other flowers. The time for drying depends on the water content of each flower. Leave the container and desiccant until cool to avoid burning your fingers.

Procedure for dessicant drying

1 Pick plant material on a dry day and process at once. Ther should be no conditioning because this increases the wate content and the aim is to remove it. Select perfect specimen just prior to maturity.

2 Cut off the stems to within 1 inch (2.5cm) of the flowe head and strip off any foliage.

3 Add a false stem or wire (unless you are intending to use , microwave oven). The stub wire can be pushed up into the bas of the stem or flower head or pushed through the centre of th flower from the top. As the flower dries it tightens on the wire For extra security the wire can have a spot of glue on the tip Tape wire and remaining stem together.

4 Find a suitable container to hold the desiccant. I use on half-pound coffee tin for single specimens and biscuit tins fo a number of flowers. The time taken by silica gel is so shor that single specimens can be processed every few days and ther is no need to process a large number at one time, which in any case uses far more desiccant.

5 Add three tablespoons of non-iodized salt to each quart o desiccant for better colour preservation. Mix well.

6 Cover the bottom of the tin with a half-inch (1cm) layer o desiccant.

7 Place the flower face up with the stem twisted or coiled up Gently pour desiccant around the flower and then between th petals using a pointed stick to separate and 'dress' them. Pour t a depth of about 1 inch (2.5cm) and shake gently. If you ca see any of the flower, add more desiccant. Spikey flowers such as lilac can be placed lengthways. It is better not to crowd flowers and to leave space for desiccant between each whe several are processed together. Make only single layers o flowers to avoid crushing. Leave the box open without a lid i it is placed in warm air. If there is any likelihood of surroundin damp air add the lid.

8 Leave the tin in a warm dry place such as an airing cupboard for as long as is necessary for the type of flower and desiccant using your own experience; for example small flowers such a primroses could be dried in silica gel in 24 hours.

9 To remove the flower pour off the desiccant in a steady stream with one hand below the tin to catch the flower if i slides out. If it is still damp and soft instead of dry and papery return it to the desiccant.

10 When dry lay the flower on top of a layer of the desiccan for 24 hours to firm up the petals. This helps to prevent them from shattering. Glue on any loose petals and brush away any desiccant in crevices, using a small watercolour paintbrush A little oil stroked on the petals with a brush adds sheen. You can then spray with a plastic coating or matt polyurethane varnish if you wish to add protection.

Pour dessicant over flower and between the petals using a pointed stick to separate them

Pour off the dessicant steadily, catching the flower as it slides out

1 Cut flowers and unfurling horse chestnut branches with houseplants.
The flowers can be replaced easily. *Arranger* Jean Taylor

2 Twists of root provide a permanent outline for a few flowers that can be changed easily.
Arranger Jean Taylor

3 A long-lasting Christmas decoration of fresh fruit and maranta leaves with artificial evergreens. *Arranger* Jean Taylor

4 Dried flowers including pink larkspur, blue delphiniums (laterals and single florets), *Helichrysum*, *Acroclinium*, nigella seedheads, grey statice and lamb's ears. *Arranger* Helen Edwards

5 Dried and fresh plant material combined for a winter arrangement of evergreens, arums and dried sedum. *Arranger* Jean Taylor

6 Pressed flower picture slightly tinted with watercolour paint.
Arranger Catherine Parry

7 A simple arrangement of summer countryside plant material with driftwood.
Arranger Richard Jeffery

8 A simple arrangement of autumn countryside plant material with driftwood.
Arranger Helen Matcham

You will find it most helpful to record results when using different desiccants, times and flowers. Stiff, brittle petals indicate that drying has been too long. A wrinkled appearance indicates that the desiccant was not heavy enough to support the petals. Damp spots on petals indicate that insufficient time was given for drying or that the desiccant was not evenly distributed.

Storage of desiccant-dried flowers

In between use keep the flowers on mounds of tissue paper in a tin, or push the wire stem into a block of dry Oasis which can be stood in a deep box such as a hat box. A little desiccant placed in the bottom of the box may help to discourage absorption of moisture, but the box should be kept in a dry room. Flowers dried in a desiccant should *not* be arranged with fresh flowers, wet Oasis or water.

Storage of dessicant

Desiccants can absorb moisture from the surrounding air as well as from plant material. It is important that before a desiccant is used all moisture is eliminated from it. This is easily done by placing it in an oven at 250° F (120°C or Mark ½) for a few hours. Some proprietary brands have built-in colour that tells you when the granules contain no water. Do be careful when handling hot desiccant because the heat is retained in the centre for a long time. After each use with plant material, it is important to dry out the desiccant by placing in a warm oven after taking flowers out.

Plants suitable for dessicant-drying

Name	Colour	Season	Method
Anemones	many colours	Spring	use open flower
Camellias	pink, white	Spring	tuck dessicant into crevices well
Carnations	many colours	all year	tuck dessicant between petals
Clematis	pink, white, mauve	Summer	use open flower
Daffodils	shades of yellow	Spring	flower open and placed upwards, light dessicant
Dahlias	many colours	Autumn	flower open and placed upwards, sift dessicant carefully between petals
Delphiniums	blue, pink mauve, cream	Summer	place lengthways
Gerberas	many colours	most of year; sold by florists	dry face upwards
Hellebores	whites, pinks, creams	Winter	face up, delicate dessicant

Name	Colour	Season	Method
Lilacs	white, cream mauve	early summer	place lengthwise in light dessicant
Marigolds	yellows, oranges, golds	Summer	face up, sift dessicent between petals
Mimosas	yellow, tiny balls	Spring	place lengthwise, light dessicant
Narcissi	as daffodils	Spring	as daffodils
Orchids	many colours	all year	face up
Pansies	many colours	Summer	face up or down
Passion flowers	white/mauve	Summer	face up – fascinating shape
Peonies	cream, pink, crimson	Summer	face up, sift dessicant between petals
Primroses	yellow	Spring	face up or down, light dessicant
Primulas	many colours	Spring	as primroses
Roses	many colours	Summer	half open as open flower. can lose petals easily. On side or face up
Zinnias	many colours	late Summer	face up, sift dessicant between petals

PRESERVING PLANT MATERIAL WITH GLYCERINE

Preserving with glycerine is a technique well known to previous generations and my mother always had an arrangement of preserved beech in our living room during the winter. For those with no source of fresh foliage a stock of preserved leaves is invaluable to combine with fresh flowers in water at any time.

There are three methods of preserving with glycerine: standing in glycerine, immersing in glycerine and mopping and spraying with glycerine. There is no shrivelling or loss of shape and the results are soft and pliable, remaining this way for years. The green colouring is lost, however, and the plant material becomes a shade of brown. However, the variations are numerous, from cream to an almost black-brown. Eucalyptus turns grey or deep purple.

Many leaves, a few flowers and some seedheads and catkins (see pages 101-102) will take up glycerine.

Standing in glycerine method

Glycerine on its own is too thick for stems to absorb and it is better mixed with water. The water evaporates from the leaves but the glycerine remains in them. The usual recipe is two parts of water to one of glycerine, stirred together well (hot water mixes more readily with glycerine). Add a teaspoon of mild disinfectant to the solution to prevent mildew at a later date.

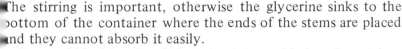

The stirring is important, otherwise the glycerine sinks to the bottom of the container where the ends of the stems are placed and they cannot absorb it easily.

Pour a 200ml bottle of glycerine into a wide-based container such as a 2-pound Kilner preserving jar; fill up the bottle twice over with hot tap water and add this to the glycerine. As well as being a good way of measuring, this sluices out the dregs remaining in the bottle. Stir the mixture well. When long branches are used they may be top heavy and the jar should be supported by wedging it in a larger container. This amount of the solution should be enough for about five 3ft (90cm) beech branches but is dependent on the number of leaves.

Preparation of plant material
Branches of foliage should be added while the solution is hot. Scrape off two inches (5cm) of bark from woody stems and slit up the ends of the stems to help absorption. Soft stems can be placed in the solution without any preparation. Remove all damaged leaves to avoid wasting glycerine on them.

Topping-up
If the solution is all taken up add some more. Leftovers can be used over and over again.

Choice of plant material
With the exception of beech, which has thin-tissued leaves, thicker-tissued foliage responds better to glycerine than thin-tissued leaves, but do try all kinds of leaf. If the glycerine is not taken up there is no waste. Here are the essential guidelines:

1 Choose leaves that are mature. July is a good month for deciduous foliage. Do not try to preserve young foliage because it flops. Leaves turning colour in autumn will not preserve as they are no longer taking up any moisture, because abscission layers have formed between the leaf stem and the twig. They are protective layers which are formed just before leaf-fall and will prevent glycerine reaching the leaf.

a. Remove crowded, damaged and lower leaves, and split and scrape the stem end before placing in the glycerine solution. b. Keep glycerine mixture at a level of 2 inches (5cm). c. Support top-heavy branches by putting the jar in a larger container

2 Cut branches with good shape.

3 Remove any superfluous or damaged branches and leaves before preserving.

4 Clean off dirt.

How long you leave foliage in glycerine is a question often asked, but one not easy to answer. Some leaves, such as beech take only a few days, others such as aspidistra can take three months. The tissue structure of the leaf makes a difference the thicker the leaf the slower it becomes charged with glycerine. I can usually tell by the change of colour; the normal green becomes very dark or a shade of brown. See the following list of plant material for appropriate timing for each. It is interesting to glycerine a few laurel leaves because you can watch the change of colour from bright green to dark brown moving up the leaf gradually.

If you find beads of glycerine on the surface of the leaves swish them in warm water containing detergent to remove the stickiness as this can mark such things as wallpaper. Dusty preserved leaves that have been in an arrangement for some time can also be washed with safety.

Immersion in glycerine method

Some leaves do not respond when stood in the glycerine solution but can be preserved when immersed in it. This is also a useful method for leaves with very short stems such as ivy leaves. Push them under the solution in a shallow dish and leave until the colour changes. Remove to drip on newspaper or tissue for a few days before wiping or washing and then storing.

Mopping and spraying with glycerine method

Some leaves such as aspidistra, monstera and large fatsia leaves are too big for the immersion method, but because of their size the tips often dry out and become brittle before preservation is complete. To avoid this mop the outside of the leaf on both sides with the solution, or spray it on occasionally while standing in the solution.

Colour change

Leaves can be lightened by standing in sunshine after preservation in glycerine and so you can have several shades of brown in one type of leaf. Beech particularly responds to this.

Another way of changing the normal brown colour is to add a dye to the glycerine solution. Any plant material that normally turns cream, such as bells-of-Ireland (*Molucella laevis*) is especially suitable, but it is interesting to experiment to achieve different effects with other plant material.

Storage

Glycerined plant material should last for years, with the occasional exception of beech which can shrivel in a very dry room.

Preserve shorter-stemmed leaves such as ivy by submerging them in the glycerine and water mixture

Mop large leaves such as those of a *monstera* with glycerine before placing the stem end in the glycerine solution

100

Leaves such as laurels, magnolias, fatsias and aspidistras will be
in the same condition ten years after preservation, which makes
them such a good investment for anyone without a garden;
they can always be combined with a few fresh flowers from a
florist. Avoid storing in a damp place or a polythene bag when
first prepared because mildew can occur, but a cardboard box
is all that is necessary for storage.

Plants suitable for preservation with glycerine;
The times taken are only a guide. Weather, time of picking and
temperature may all affect the process. Unless otherwise indic-
ated, stand stems in glycerine solution.

Leaf Name	Weeks	Colour	Method
Aspidistra	12	beige	mop
Atriplex	½	beige	
Beech, green	1-2	shades of brown	
Bergenia	3-4	dark brown	immerse
Box	3-4	beige	
Broom	2	almost black	
Camellia	4	dark brown, tough, shiny	
Choisya	3	light beige	
Contoneaster	2-4	colour varies with type	
Elaeagnus	4-6	variegation is lost	
Fatsia	2-6	mid-brown	mop or submerge
Ferns	2	mid-brown	pick when spores show
Grevillea	2	colour varies	
Ivy	2-3	mid-brown	mop or submerge
Hellebore	2-3	light brown	
Hornbeam	2-3	mid-brown	
Laurel	2-3	very tough, dark brown	
Magnolia	3-4	tough, dark brown	
Mahonia	2-3	light brown	
Oak	2	light brown	
Pittosporum	2	mid-brown	
Rhododendron	2	mid-brown	single leaves better
Rose	2	dark green	use woody stem
Rubber plant	4	mid-to dark brown	mop or submerge
Spotted laurel	3	variegation lost, dark brown	
Sweet chestnut	1-2	light brown	single leaves better
Whitebeam	2	brown with grey underside	shrivels easily

Other plant material suitable for preservation with glycerine

Name	Weeks	Colour	Method
Garrya elliptica catkins	3	mid-brown	treat in spring
Hornbeam seeds	2-3	mid-brown	remove leaves
Hydrangea flowers	2	light brown	use woody stems
Irish seed pods	2	mid-brown	
Lime flowers	2-3	light brown	remove leaves
Old-man's-beard	2	light brown	treat before flowers open
Pussy willow catkins	2	grey-brown	treat when silky
Sea-holly flowers	2-3	light brown	
Teasels	3	beige	treat when green

FALSE STEMS FOR DRIED AND PRESERVED PLANT MATERIAL

The natural stems with rigid structure of such plants as delphiniums and achilleas can be used in an arrangement and support the flower perfectly. However, some stems shrivel up during the drying process or are too short to use in an arrangement. In this case a false stem is necessary.

Florists often wire fresh flowers to hold them in position in bouquets and other designs, although for normal home flower arrangements this is not necessary except when providing a stem for a dried flower. It is therefore useful to know a little about the technique of wiring. The wires used for false stems are called stub wires and they come in a number of lengths and gauges. These now conform to the metric system of measurement. I have never found it a necessity to know gauges and have gone by the 'feel' of the wire, its weight, length and malleability. Some wires are so strong that they cannot be bent gracefully and are only suitable for use as straight stems. Stub wires are sold by florists and flower club sales tables. A large heavier flower such as a dried dahlia will need a stronger stem than a small dried strawflower. Generally speaking 30 gauge (0.32mm) is suitable for light flowers and 20 gauge (0.90mm) for heavier ones. The higher the gauge number the lighter the wire. I would suggest you buy an assortment in a long length; they are available from 3½-18 inches (9-45cm). If a wire is too long it can be cut and the remainder used for another flower.

The wires can soon become rusty and should therefore be stored in a polythene bag that has been wiped lightly inside with oil.

Some methods of wiring

Flowers

It is better to wire a flower when fresh before the centre becomes hard during drying.

1 For flowers with a strong centre such as strawflower (*Helichrysum*) dried naturally in air, or a single dahlia dried in a dessicant, push a stub wire through the centre until the tip is concealed; as the flower dries it will tighten on the wire.

2 For perfect security you can turn over a small hook before drawing the wire through the centre of the flower.

3 Flowers with short, rather thick stems of about 1-2 inches (2.5-5cm) that have been cut to bury in a desiccant, such as a rose, can have a stub wire pushed into the stem which will tighten on the wire as it dries.

4 Flowers with large seedboxes such as a carnation or a rose, or flowers that are thick at the base like a camellia, can have two wires pushed at right angles through the seedbox or the base of the flower. Turn down the wires and twist one end around the other three. Use as few twists as possible to keep the bulk to a minimum. Alternatively, use very thin wire to bind the wires together, making a slimmer stem.

Push wire down into stem until hook disappears in the flower centre

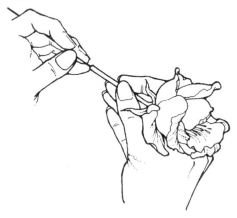

Above Insert wire into flowers with short, thick stems

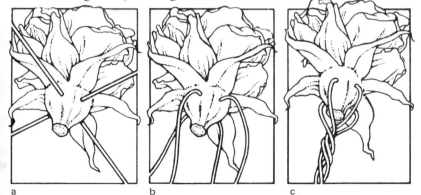

a   b   c

Left   a. Insert two wires at right angles into base of the flower's seedbox. b. Turn down wires c. Twist wires round each other

5 Small flowers such as violets and primroses can be grouped together and bound with fine flexible wire such as fuse wire.

6 Bell-shaped flowers such as hyacinth florets can be threaded on a wire, like beads, to make a spray.

Leaves

Preserved leaves are better wired *after* treatment.

1 The simplest method is to lay a stub wire next to the mid-rib on the back of a leaf and then to Sellotape it in place.

2 Using a stub wire take a 'stitch' across the mid-rib of a leaf about 1 inch (2.5cm) above its base. Turn down the ends of the wire and twist one end around the other and around the remaining leaf. The 'stitch' should be as unobtrusive as possible from the front.

Thread bell-shaped flowers on a wire to make a spray

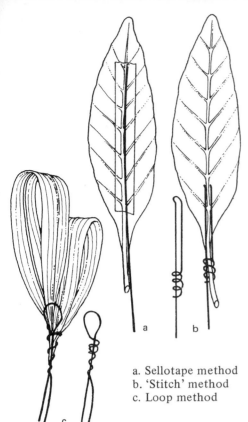

a. Sellotape method
b. 'Stitch' method
c. Loop method

3 Make a loop of wire and lay it against the back of the leaf about one-third of the way up. Twist one end around the other end and the leaf stem.

Pine cones

Two stub wires provide the most satisfactory stem because when only one is used the cone still remains wobbly. Push the stub wires into the lower part of the cone so that they are parallel. Twist the ends together on either side and then bend them downwards and twist all together to make a single stem.

Gourds, avocados and pomegranates

Gourds, avocados and pomegranates cannot be wired without making a hole. I am reluctant to do this and normally use them without an artificial stem by grouping them at the base of an arrangement. Avocados and pomegranates become very hard when dry and if you need a stem a stub wire should be inserted before drying. Gourds become hollow and a wire inserted will wobble about; a wooden meat skewer glued where it enters the gourd is more secure. Lotus seedpods are normally sold ready wired.

Concealing wires

Stub wires are unattractive and should be covered for normal use, although when making a plaque of dried plant material you will be able to conceal the wires because the plant material is packed closely together.

1 Slip the wire into a dried hollow stem from another plant. It is helpful to make a collection of these. Many grasses and herbaceous plants have hollow stems that can be dried. These usually provide a straight stem.

2 For a flexible stem it is better to bind the wire with florist's tape (also called gutta-percha). This is stretchable tape that clings to itself. Start by winding a small amount around the top of the stem (natural or wire) at right angles, and as soon as it feels secure start to stretch the tape at an angle, holding the flower in one hand and twisting it round so that the tape covers the wire. Pinch the tape with your warm fingers to make it

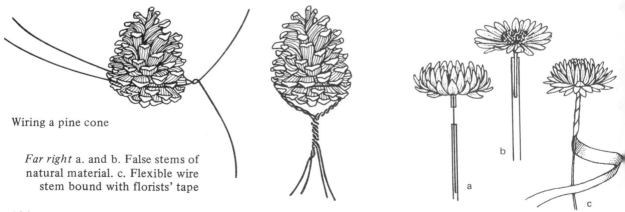

Wiring a pine cone

Far right a. and b. False stems of natural material. c. Flexible wire stem bound with florists' tape

47 Dried lotus seedpods arranged with a stem of single chrysanthemums for an economical arrangement. (*Arranger* Madge Green)

stick together. When you come to the end of the wire break off the tape. You may find it necessary to twist around a short length of fuse wire so that the tape does not unravel.

Glueing on branches and twigs

Dried flowers can be glued on to branches and slender twigs. These stems will not be as flexible as wire but will look natural and can be chosen for their attractive curves. Real stems are better not taped like wire but left in their natural condition. They could be painted a shade of green to look like a fresh flower stem.

USING DRIED AND PRESERVED PLANT MATERIAL

So many people think of dried arrangements as lacking bright colouring, so when making arrangements or other decorations

48 This fascinating branch covered
in grey-green lichen requires no
additional plant material. With
its windswept lines it would make
a good arrangement for March.
(*Arranger* Edith Brack)

do try to add colours other than brown. Although designs can
look very beautiful in shades of brown, it is a pity not to take
advantage of the lovely colourings that can be retained such as
blue delphiniums and pink larkspur dried quickly in the airing
cupboard to retain colour, yellow achilleas and purple statice.

Arrangements

Dried and preserved plant material

You can make an arrangement entirely of dried flowers and
preserved leaves as a semi-permanent decoration. In this case no
water or water-retaining foam should be used and the mechanics
should be dry. You can use dry Oasis, wire netting, a pinholder
or any of the compounds such as Plasticine or Florafix. Some
of these remain soft and the stems can be removed. Others set
hard and the arrangement is permanent unless the stems are cut
away from the block. Dry Oasis is very light and an arrangement
can be toppled over easily by the weight of the plant material.

This is avoidable if the Oasis fits the container exactly or if Oasis tape or a cap of wire netting, wired to the container, is used over the foam.

All glycerined foliage can be used with fresh flowers in water or soaked foam at any time and it is invaluable for winter arrangements or for people without gardens from which to cut leaves. Foliage to preserve can be gleaned from people with gardens or from the countryside during the summer. It then provides a background for a few fresh flowers at any time. The stem ends can be bound or dried out from time to time as for dried plant material.

Dried and fresh plant material

Water or water-retaining foam is necessary for fresh flowers, so the dried flowers combined with them must be those with rigid, strong stems and flower tissue, otherwise they will re-absorb moisture. Achillea, artichokes and lotus seedpods are good examples. Others, such as lady's mantle (*Alchemilla mollis*), with delicate tissue will soon collapse.

The ends of natural stems can become soft and sometimes mouldy, but this can be avoided by taping the ends with gutta-percha, or by drying out the stems between use in arrangements;

Wall hangings

Pictures, plaques and swags can be made with dried and pre-served plant material for permanent decorations in a variety of sizes, shapes and styles. Plant material preserved in silica

49 *Left* A picture in a recessed frame of pressed and dried plant material. (*Arranger* Renee Mottershead)

50 Brown glycerined and dried plant material for an unglazed picture on natural-coloured hessian. The plant material is slightly sprayed with gold and includes split curled bean pods, cedar cones, helichrysums, seed pods of *Phormium tenax* and *Clematis montana,* clayxes of bells-of-Ireland. (*Arranger* Doris Hickson)

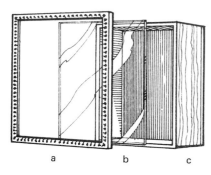

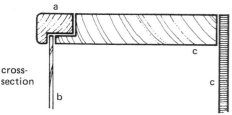

cross-
section

a. Picture moulding. b. glass. c. deep picture box attached to hardboard back

gel can be used in pictures under glass because they are protected from any surrounding moisture, but plaques and swags without protection should be made from less fragile material.

Pictures

These differ from pressed flower pictures because the plant material is three-dimensional and placed behind raised glass. Special recessed frames can be bought quite easily for this purpose. You can, however, make your own by boxing the back of a frame with batten so that it has at least a 2 inch (5cm) gap between the background and the glass. Round and oval recessed frames can be bought as well as rectangular and square ones, but when making your own oval or circular recessed frame you need to bend stiff cardboard to form the walls of the recess.

The recess can be covered with fabric glued to the surface before adding the dried plant material. Decorator's size is a reliable glue for covering boards with fabric. Using a paintbrush cover the board with the size, allow it to dry, then size thoroughly again. Press on the fabric using a clean, dry duster and continue to press for some time. Cotton-backed fabrics are the easiest to use and velvet, hessian and fine linen are effective. Soft colours, such as dove grey, grey-blues and greens, and browns enhance the plant material better than strong colours.

Do not glue on the plant material until you are satisfied with the design and then use a latex glue (non-stringing Dufix, Copydex or Clam) or Uhu, being careful not to get the glue on to the background by placing the glue on the plant material away from the frame. Only a touch is necessary. An alternative to glueing on each piece of plant material is to insert the stems into a mound of slow-drying adhesive placed on the background.

It is not necessary to insert glass for a picture can be hung without it, but glass does protect the plant material from dust.

Plaques

A plaque is usually described as a decoration with a visible background, and is without glass. This can be made of wood framed or unframed; the wood can be left in the natural state, or stained or varnished, or it can be hardboard covered with fabric. Even heavy cardboard is suitable. Some people call this type of decoration a collage or montage. To achieve a very professional fabric background:

Preparation of base

1 Cut a piece of hardboard to the desired shape to use for a base.

2 Cut a piece of velvet to the same shape but with an extra allowance of one half inch (1cm) to turn on to the reverse side.

3 Cut Terylene wadding, the size and shape of the hardboard,

51 Velvet and silk plaque made from dried plant material. (*Arranger* Audrey Caldwell)

108

52 Flowers of many colours dried in silica gel and arranged in the manner of a Flemish flower painting. The rayon slub-silk mount is stuck on hardboard. (*Arranger* M. Rice-Oxley)

53 Seascape, a plaque using broom, dried seedpods, skeletonised magnolia leaves and a shell on blue felt. The poppy seedheads at the base are touched with water-based paint. (*Arranger* Emma Armsworth)

to make a soft padding between the fabric and the hardboard (for a flat effect omit wadding).

4 Glue the edge of the fabric using Copydex. It is more satisfactory to use a plastic-nozzled container instead of a brush to apply the glue because this type of glue congeals quickly on a brush. Leave a few minutes for the glue to become tacky before covering the board and wadding.

5 Cover a second, smaller hardboard shape with a toning silk in the same way. Glue this centrally on the velvet-covered plaque. Take great care at this stage.

6 When the glue has set, encircle the oval with matching silk cord or metallic braid and make a bow at the base of the oval to hide the join, using the same cord or braid.

7 Add a loop of cord at the top, glueing it to the board, to hang the plaque.

8 Cover the reverse side of the plaque with felt cut to shape.

Simpler backgrounds

Paint a piece of hardboard with a matt soft-coloured paint (emulsion is suitable). Edge the board with a wooden edging or beading from a do-it-yourself shop. Add hooks and wire on the back for hanging. Cover a piece of hardboard with fabric,

54 Collage using seeds and tiny dried flowers in beige, green and orange on brown linen. (*Arranger* Kit Gasser)

55 *Right* An owl made with many different seeds, including some that give a feathery effect. (*Arranger* Joan Reffel)

such as linen, hessian or velvet, and add a frame if you wish. Cork sheeting and strawcloth are alternatives. Use an existing frame, omitting the glass and covering the backing with fabric.

Seed collage

Seeds come in a large range of colours, sizes, shapes and textures. A seed warehouse is the ideal place to search, but there are fascinating seeds to be found in corn chandlers, supermarkets, pet food suppliers, your own garden and the countryside. One's own kitchen can supply a good variety, and retail seedsmen have plenty of interesting vegetable seeds. The backing for a seed collage can be the usual hardboard, painted or covered in fabric, framed or unframed. Velvets, silks and satins are not as satisfactory with seeds as hessian, linen or cotton fabrics. For details of preparation see pages 108-109.

A natural, stylized or abstract design can be planned and it is advisable to draw out the design on paper beforehand, using coloured pens or crayons. The seeds can be grouped in masses of one variety or can be used singly or in small groups.

Tweezers make it easier to work with small seeds and a compartmented box such as those sold for storing nails, or a tray of small receptacles for the different types of seed makes the choosing much easier than leaving them in various paper bags. Copydex, Clam or Pritt are used by arrangers, but any adhesive that does not 'string' is suitable. Seed collage is an interesting activity for children as well as adults, especially if they collect their own seeds.

Suitable seeds for seed collage

Angelica	Laburnum	Peppercorns
Beans (in brown, black, red, green)	(poisonous)	Pomegranate
	Lentils	Rice (long grain)
Coffee beans	Marigold	Split peas
Coriander	Melon	Sunflower (parrot food)
Gourd	Mustard	Vegetable marrow (cream)
Hollyhock	Parsnip	

Swags

A swag is described as having no visible backing. However, a strong backing is necessary on which to attach the plant material. Inspiration can be obtained through a study of Grinling Gibbons wood carvings. The backing can be of shaped hardboard or pegboard, which has useful holes through which wires can be pushed for securing plant material. No painting or covering is necessary because it is concealed.

Plant material can be glued on using a quick-drying adhesive and a three-dimensional effect can be achieved by building up plant material, one piece in front of another. Felt on the back can be a protection for a wall if many wires are used.

Cones

A favourite decoration using dried plant material is a cone, especially at Christmas time. Ready-shaped dry Oasis is available and it is easy to push wires into it. A backing of preserved leaves pinned flat on to the cone to begin with is a help because the cone is then concealed before you add other plant material. The wires can go through the leaves.

Another method is to use wire netting of half-inch (1 cm) mesh in a cone shape filled with moss. Allow the moss to dry completely before adding dried plant material.

The completed cone can be used flat on a fabric-covered cakeboard, or set on a container with a stem. Alternatively you can push a dowel into the base and set the other end in a plastic pot of plaster of Paris for a tree effect. Remember that plaster of Paris sets in a few minutes.

Garlands

A garland of dried plant material with a light dusting of gold spray paint is lovely at Christmas. It is daintier in appearance if the garland is kept narrow. A lampshade ring or a coat hanger bound with florist's tape or with bias binding makes a good base. Wire on the plant material and add one or more bows.

Flower paperweights

Clear casting kits for making paperweights (and other objects) are available from suppliers of glassfibre or hobby shops.

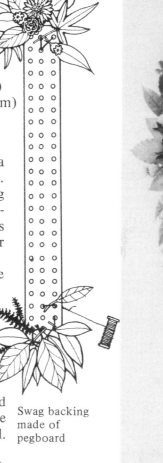

Swag backing made of pegboard

56 A dried plant material swag can enhance a wall and be a decorative feature. This includes pine cones, poppy seedheads and glycerined foliage. (*Arranger* Rennee Mottershead)

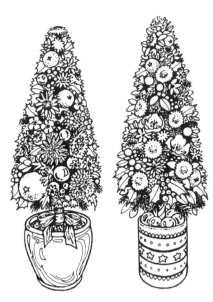

Christmas decorations using dried plant material pinned onto cone base or wire netting

Moulds are supplied but you may find cheap glasses are more satisfactory. The work is quite messy and surfaces should be well-covered with newspaper before you start. Moulds should be well polished with release wax so that the finished paper-weights can be removed easily. The paperweight is built up in quarter-inch layers and each layer must set before the next one is poured in (follow manufacturer's instructions carefully). Dried flowers should be added on to a tacky layer before it sets, remembering that you are working upside down and the bottom of the mould will be the top of the paperweight. Continue to add resin and dried plant material until the mould is full and then leave for twenty-four hours.

To remove the paperweight run a knife around the top layer to release the pressure, then place the mould into a bowl of hot water to heat up. Leave for 15 minutes and then repeat with cold water. This expands and contracts the paperweight, which should slide out with a twist. Felt or Fablon can be stuck to the base and rough edges at the bottom can be sandpapered.

After some practice you may like to cast resin in panels to set in wooden frames. These can be joined together to make a screen, each with a design of dried plant material. With a light behind the screen the effect is quite ethereal.

Left Bind lampshade ring or coat hanger with tape. Add pine cones, glycerined leaves, dried flowers and a ribbon

Below a. Place the dried flower upside down on a tacky layer of resin in the mould. b. Build up the resin in ¼ inch (6mm) layers. c. Remove the paperweight after 24 hours

a

b

c

8 DRIFTWOOD

Nothing rivals driftwood for making a large arrangement with only a few flowers and leaves. It is said that you either love or hate driftwood, and there are no half measures. The setting in which you normally place flower arrangements usually influences your feelings about it. It certainly suits all modern houses, but if you have a home full of choice antiques, driftwood may seem too rustic in appearance. Untreated it seems more suitable for a sun room or porch, although when cleaned and polished some pieces can look surprisingly elegant.

Driftwood also changes its character according to the way in which it is used, and there are many styles. Wood can be used alone like modern sculpture or combined with flowers, foliage, plants or bulbs. It can be the main feature of a design or play a lesser part. It can be used in traditional or modern, and dried or fresh arrangements.

The merits of driftwood are that it costs nothing; it can stretch a few flowers to make a large but economical arrangement and, if you wish, it can be left in place almost permanently with an occasional change of flowers. Every piece is unique, timeless and durable. Its disadvantages are that it needs some preparation before it can be used and it can be difficult to store because it is often bulky with irregular projections.

WHAT IS DRIFTWOOD?

A dictionary definition is 'wood floating on, or cast ashore by, the water', but flower arrangers call any wood that has been weathered by the elements 'driftwood'. It has been shaped by wind, water and rock, aged by the seasons and coloured according to the type of wood it is and its exposure to sunshine. For the purpose of competitive flower arrangement shows it is usually classified as dried plant material.

This generally descriptive term covers chunks of wood of many sizes — stumps, branches, bark, roots and crosscuts — from all types of tree, woody shrubs and climbers. But it is not a term normally used for a branch that can produce new buds.

57 Bleached white driftwood found on a Norfolk beach combined with a single rose. Any round flower or flowers could be substituted. (*Arranger* Edith Brack)

58 *Right* Blackened burnt gorse with yellow double tulips (*Arranger* Barbara Thexton)

WHERE TO FIND DRIFTWOOD

Perhaps it is the anticipation and the excitement of finding interesting pieces that grips the lover of driftwood. It can be found in the countryside, on lake shores, on river banks and beds, and on the sea coast — almost anywhere in the world. Many a piece found abroad has been brought home by air with care that is not lavished on normal luggage.

Some shops sell wood already cleaned and ready to use. It may also be found on construction sites where trees and stumps are being removed, and on ground where there has been a bonfire.

Pieces found inland are not often worth carrying home because they are likely to be rotting. The best wood is usually found where there is woodland close to water. Trees and sections

114

of trees fall into the water which wears off the softer, flimsier parts, leaving the hard core to be washed ashore on a beach or lakeside. The tides also yield interesting wood from ships, small boats and parts of breakwaters and pier staging. Grey wood, i.e. brown wood bleached by the sun, is normally found in exposed places where there is strong sunlight.

In some countries, such as the British Isles, the late winter, especially after storms, is the best time to look for wood; during summer it becomes hidden by undergrowth. In more equable climates you can search at any time, but in cold regions with heavy snow, summer is the only time available.

WHAT TO LOOK FOR

Rotting and worm-eaten wood is not worth carrying home because it is unpleasant to have around and will disintegrate in time. Hard wood with only a few soft parts (which are removable) is the most satisfactory.

Look first for hard wood and then study the shape. Many pieces are straight and uninteresting and should be discarded, but remember that the form can sometimes be modified by removing some projections to improve the shape or glueing several pieces together. To avoid carrying home useless pieces give each one a test by holding it against the light to study the shape. Turn it in different directions but do not be concerned about lack of stability because this can be remedied.

Left Use a wire brush and knife to ease out soft wood in a piece of driftwood

PREPARATION OF DRIFTWOOD

Find a piece of wood
Clean it by washing or scrubbing
Dry it
Remove soft and broken wood
Alter the shape
Decide the mechanics and make
    any necessary modifications
Add colour if desired
Polish

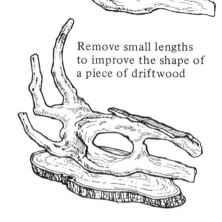

Remove small lengths to improve the shape of a piece of driftwood

Cleaning

Rarely is a piece of wood perfectly clean, and washing does no harm. It is also more pleasant to have in your home when all dust, dirt and appendages such as moss and creepy-crawlies have been removed. If you think it necessary, use some disinfectant in the washing water. Most wood can be scrubbed, but I would not advise vigorous scrubbing of grey wood because the grey is on the surface only and can be easily scraped off.

Sunshine or an airing cupboard dry wood quickly, but in time it will dry anywhere indoors. After washing and drying, further grooming is usually necessary to remove broken pieces and the soft wood remaining in crevices. This job is better done

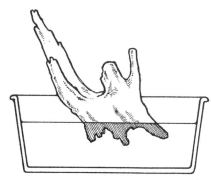

Form a sawing line by holding
a piece of driftwood in water

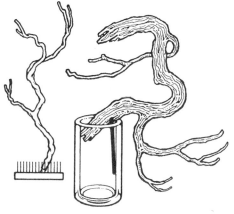

Left Impale a slender piece of wood
on a pinholder

Above Add dowel stick peg-leg
to hold driftwood in position

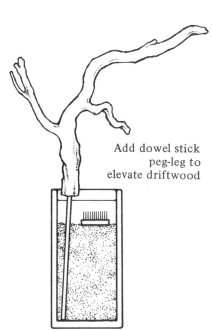

Add dowel stick
peg-leg to
elevate driftwood

out-of-doors or in an outhouse because it can be dusty. Use a small chisel and a pointed implement to ease out soft wood. A wire brush is excellent for removing a soft crumbling surface and getting down to the inner hard wood, but again avoid brushing grey wood. This grooming takes time but it is worthwhile because you will end with a well-finished piece of wood that is a pleasure to see.

Altering the shape

For a few days study the shape of the wood from a number of angles. I stand it in some place that I often pass during the day and this helps to make the final evaluation. Avoid sawing off large pieces if possible because it leaves a scar which can be hard to camouflage, although the removal of smaller lengths can streamline the shape.

You can also relocate sections to improve height, shape or balance (the join is hardly noticeable when the sections are from the same piece of wood). Use a wood glue as a bonding agent, or join sections by inserting a strong metal rod or a dowel into holes drilled in each piece. If the rods are a good fit glue is unnecessary, and large, joined constructions can be taken apart for storage or transport. Several pieces of similar wood can be joined to make a most imposing 'sculpture'.

Mechanics

It is advisable to consider how to support the wood at this stage in case any more sawing or joining is necessary before adding colour or polish. There are a number of ways of holding a piece of driftwood in position firmly. The ideal wood is self-supporting, but it is not often that one finds such a piece.

Sometimes levelling the bottom eliminates the need for further mechanics. To mark a sawing line dip the wood, held at the desired angle, into a sink of water. Hold it so that a tidemark is formed. Alternatively ask someone to draw a chalk line just above the water level.

Wedges and pinholes

You can also level wood by adding a wedge instead of sawing away sections. Glue, screw or nail on the wedge.

A slender piece of wood can be impaled on a pinholder; if this is difficult, slit the stem end.

Peg-legs

Do-it-yourself shops sell dowel sticks in a number of thicknesses, and lengths can be used as 'legs' to support wood in a desired position. Drill a hole in the wood of the same diameter as the dowel and then glue it in. It is important to fix the dowel at the correct angle and this needs care.

A peg-leg of dowel is useful when placing wood in a container. It can be hooked into the container leaving the wood on the outside. Some chunks have natural appendages that will hook into a container, so try the wood in different positions before sawing off all the projections.

A wooden dowel or a metal rod can be used to elevate driftwood by inserting one end into the driftwood and the other into a mounting block as used to display sculpture, with which it has similarity.

Driftwood screwed on to a mounting block by means of a counter-sunk screw

Bases for support

A base made of wood and about half an inch (1cm) thick makes an excellent support. It can be a crosscut of driftwood or a piece of wood from a do-it-yourself shop sawn to a pattern you have supplied. The heavier the wood the broader must be the base. A screw can be inserted through the base from underneath and countersunk so that furniture is not scratched. A hole of the same diameter should then be drilled in the bottom of the wood so that it can be twisted on to the base screw when you wish to use it.

Heavier pieces of wood may not be sufficiently supported by one screw, and an alternative method is to hammer a ring of long nails into the base so that the end of the wood can be slotted in. This necessitates plant material being used to conceal the nails. The base can be sanded, stained and polished, or it can be painted.

Heavy piece of wood held in place by a ring of nails

Plaster of Paris

Plaster of Paris gives firm support. Heavy driftwood can be inserted into an empty paint can full of plaster. The can needs to be painted a dull colour and can be concealed with plant material. This is a permanent support and the only method of releasing the wood is by hammering off the plaster.

Lighter pieces of wood can be supported by a lump of plaster without a can. The plaster can be concealed with moss or stones. If it is to be used in water, varnish the plaster to seal it.

Plaster of Paris is sold in powder form by chemists, drug stores and paint shops. It is easy to work with but sets in a few minutes when mixed with water, so speed is essential.

If you are going to support your piece of driftwood in a can, pour in the powder, add water and stir. As soon as it is similar to thick, whipped cream add the wood, but be careful to hold it at the correct angle because once the plaster sets it cannot be moved. When not using a can, mix the plaster in the same way in a dispensable container, pour it on to a polythene sheet and mound it up as it sets, quickly inserting the wood and continuing to mound.

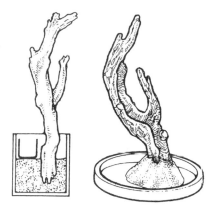

Left Heavy piece of wood supported in a paint can full of plaster of Paris

Right Lighter piece of wood supported by a lump of plaster of Paris at the base

Commercial devices

From time to time new devices for holding driftwood in position arrive on the market. There is a flat metal disc with an embedded screw which can be inserted into the end of the wood, and a clamp with a screw which is especially suitable for branches, roots and slender stems. Some clamps have an inverted pin-holder on the base which fits down firmly on to a normal

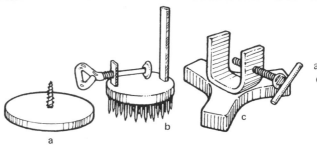

a. Lead disc with embedded screw
b. Inverted pin-holder clamp
c. Heavy clamp with screw

59 Five pieces of driftwood screwed together and painted with matt black paint, mounted on a brass rod and block of wood with a fresh white carnation in a tube of water. (*Arranger* Patricia de Meyer)

pinholder. Neither the disc nor the clamp will hold heavy pieces, which are better supported by a base or plaster of Paris. Keep a look-out in florist's, flower club sales' tables and garden centres for the latest device.

Mechanics to avoid

Plasticine is not strong enough to hold wood, for when it becomes warm it can soften and cause the wood to slip out.

Oasis is suitable for very light wood, but not for heavy pieces or broad stems because it breaks away. It is possible to use Oasis for light wood only in conjunction with a cap of wire netting as a second support.

Colouring driftwood

Most driftwood has a beautiful natural colour and needs no additional artificial colouring, but occasionally this can improve the appearance, and sometimes a special colour effect may be wanted.

Wood stain

There are many colours, which are shown on the outside of each tin. It is advisable first to try some on a section of the driftwood that is not obvious or on a piece cut off. Stain adds colour but not shine. Paint it on carefully and evenly.

Shoe polish

Polishes can add colour as well as a sheen and some of the browns are especially effective. Rub it in with a rag or small brush and then, after a few hours, polish with a clean rag or brush. More than one coat can be applied.

Paint

Black and white matt paint, such as emulsion, is effective for modern designs, but other colours can also be used. Paint tends to dull the texture and flatten the appearance of wood, but some interesting effects can be obtained. Glossy paint can be too hard and eye-catching, but lovely results can be obtained by spray-painting with more than one colour or by highlighting a colour with silver, gold or copper spray paint. Rubbing off some of the paint with a rag or steel wool while it is still wet can also give interesting results. Consider well before you paint because it is tedious or impossible to remove.

Chalk

This rubs or washes off easily but is useful when a temporary change of colour is needed.

Linseed oil

This preserves wood but darkens it. No shine is added by the oil.

Bleach

Some wood is improved by bleaching. Soak the wood for several hours in a bucket of water containing half a bottle of bleach. Rinse and dry. However, bleach is inclined to yellow the wood in addition to lightening it.

Polishing driftwood

Wax

A light waxing, using furniture wax or colourless shoe polish, improves most wood with the exception of grey or pale wood which it will darken. Rub on the wax liberally. Leave overnight and then polish with a clean rag or brush. Some pieces of wood are so intricate in form that waxing is difficult and they are better left natural or given a protective spray of matt polyurethane.

Varnish

Shiny varnish tends to spoil the texture of natural wood, although it does protect it. Matt polyurethane protects without loss, but this makes later waxing less effective.

USES FOR DRIFTWOOD

Driftwood-and-flower arrangements

Does wood harmonise with any plant material? Different countries associate wood with different flowers. In the British Isles you rarely see driftwood used with orchids, but in America this combination is often seen. In South Africa wood is used for large-scale dramatic designs; in Britain it is a favourite component for naturalistic and wild flower arrangements.

It does seem that wood is compatible with all types and combinations of plant material. Its bold form is excellent with fruit; it can be combined most successfully with leaves. Seed-heads, fresh flowers and dried and perserved plant material can all be used with success. Whatever plant material is used do make sure the driftwood remains a feature and is not hidden behind a mass of flowers or leaves, otherwise there is no point in using it.

For economical arrangement nothing is easier than combining an interesting, well-groomed piece of wood, firmly held in its mechanics, with two or three flowers and some leaves. These can be placed at the foot of the wood in a concealed container, or wood, flowers and foliage can be arranged in a decorative container together.

When a concealed container is used the arrangement normally looks more finished when a base is placed under all the components. A simple guideline is two flowers in a round or near-

60 A summer arrangement of grey-grained driftwood, four feet high, and two huge pink peonies. (*Arranger* Edith Brack)

round shape and several leaves, which are related in scale to the flowers, to soften the appearance of the design.

Driftwood can often be left in position, changing flowers when necessary. It makes an ideal semi-permanent outline.

For height

There are many times when long-stemmed flowers or leaves are not obtainable and yet you feel that height is necessary for the setting of an arrangement. One or more branches or roots of driftwood, or slender pieces of tree trunk, can supply the desired height. This is an especially effective use of wood in the spring because most bulb flowers have short stems. In addition the leafless branch resembles the bare trees of early spring and gives a seasonal association. Pot-et-fleur often lack height so driftwood, pushed well down into the compost, can add necessary height.

When branches are used for height they often look better after pruning. This gives more importance to the vertical appearance. Such branches are called in design terms 'line plant material'.

Driftwood as a cover-up

A collection of small pieces of hard wood or bark is of great value, even if you are not a lover of larger pieces. One or more can be placed over or around the mechanics of an arrangement to conceal them – they give a cleaner appearance to a design than an excess of leaves. Small pieces of wood can be used to hide a pinholder within a container, especially a wide, shallow dish. Water does no harm. They are also invaluable for concealing a utility container, such as a food tin or plastic dish, used on a base.

Collect a number of varying colours and shapes to provide plenty of choice for your arrangements. Some can be left in their natural state, others painted, polished or stained. Pieces with a gentle curve are a good find because they fit closely around mechanics.

Driftwood bases

Flat pieces of wood and crosscuts from tree trunks make excellent bases on which to stand containers or on which to support taller lengths of wood. They really must be flat, however, otherwise there will be problems with both actual and visual balance.

It is not easy to cut a narrow crosscut but do your best to obtain one about ½-1 inch (1-2.5cm) deep. Any deeper base is visually very heavy and bulky to use. Sometimes workmen sawing down trees will cut off a slice for you.

Clean, sand, stain and polish or paint the wood or, after cleaning, leave it natural, depending on the desired effect. Felt can be glued to the underside to avoid scratching table

Pieces of driftwood used to conceal
a container

61 Damp moss on a rough wood
slice forms a base for a simple landscape. The two carved deer shelter
under a manzanita 'tree' and bushes
of golden cupressus and juniper.
(*Arranger* Dorothy Haworth)

tops. Polished pieces, especially of wood such as walnut, can look quite beautiful with a formal container. Unpolished slices are harmonious with arrangements of wild flowers or in landscape designs.

Driftwood sculpture

A really fine piece of driftwood makes an excellent permanent feature in a room, and it is always a talking point. It is worth going to considerable trouble, if you find a piece with a beautiful shape and texture, to clean and polish it. It can be screwed or pinned to a plinth or flat base which has been painted or polished. A light effect is achieved by mounting the wood with a narrow part touching the base. Some pieces can stand alone without a base and look attractive in a hearth, but make sure no one burns them as firewood!

Driftwood containers

Large chunks of wood often have a cavity that can be increased in size or reshaped to make a space big enough to hold a concealed container for water and mechanics. A level base is essential to avoid water spillage.

Natural wood containers have an affinity with flowers. They can be used for an elegant effect if stained and polished and can be stood on an antique or raised stand. Unpolished they are more suitable for naturalistic arrangements, and a tree stump makes a delightful container for spring flowers with a longer piece of wood for height.

Driftwood makes an attractive table centrepiece for a meal out-of-doors. In this case, if people are not to be put off their food by the sight of dirty, insect-infested wood, it is essential to clean it thoroughly and wax it.

Driftwood 'trees'

Landscape designs are copies of natural scenes. The relative scale of everything in the arrangement must be the same as the natural scale of life. A tree can be represented by a small driftwood branch, although some searching may be necessary to find a piece that has the necessary shape.

Plaques and pictures

A small but interesting twist of branch or root can be used in a plaque of dried plant material. Heavy or bulky pieces should be avoided because of their weight.

Peeled bark, such as that of silver birch which can be very thin, can make an abstract plaque, or if paper-thin, a picture. It can be used for its texture (the sides are often different), its colouring, which is usually subtle, and its shape. It is not advisable to break it off a tree as this can harm it, but you will often find pieces already peeling away or lying at the base of the tree.

Display stands

Shop owners have found that driftwood makes an interesting support on which to display their goods. Pieces with many smaller offshoots can be mounted on a base and used for rings, bracelets and necklaces.

9 PRESSED FLOWER DECORATIONS

A pressed flower picture can last so long that it becomes a family heirloom. But there are other ways to use plant material that has been gleaned and pressed to last for years. You can decorate brooches, tablemats, fingerplates for doors, trinket boxes, calendars and greeting cards, for your own use or to give as presents. Anything made with pressed flowers is usually highly decorative and a source of great interest to your friends and visitors.

Pressing is not new; many of us have opened an old book and a little pressed flower has fallen out, but recently pressing has become more skilled and the making of pictures extremely popular. For many people it is one of the most pleasurable activities in flower arrangement, and one that produces charming, long-lasting results with little effort and expense.

There is one drawback that should be mentioned in case of eventual disappointment — some colours do not stay true and all colours fade in time. This can be delayed by keeping the flowers out of strong light and by choosing colours that change less readily than others (see page 127). Some people add touches of watercolour paint to retain colour at the time of making a picture. But I do not find the faded colours unattractive and the soft beiges, creams and greys have their own subtle beauty for many people.

EQUIPMENT FOR PRESSING

You will need something with which to press the plant material. Heavy books and bricks are often used. If you wish to try a heavy weight such as a book all you will need is blotting paper. This both absorbs water and protects the pages of the book. But I think it is well worth while buying a press made for the purpose. Get the largest you can find. It is well worth the extra money because a press is soon filled and the plant material cannot be removed for several months. I find that two large presses provide me with plenty of plant material. Blotting paper and cardboard are sold with commercial presses. The results are much better than those obtained with plants pressed under weight because the plant material becomes paper thin and does not wrinkle.

62 The colours have faded to cream and brown with grey but the design is still very attractive. (*Arranger* Catherine Parry)

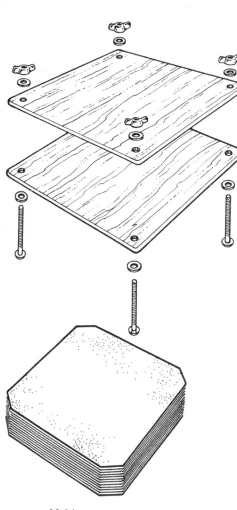

Making a press

A press is not difficult to make if you wish to save money.

You will need

2 pieces of thick plywood or chipboard, about 10 inches (25 cm) square

10 sheets of thick cardboard cut to 10 inches (25 cm) square

18 sheets of blotting paper of similar size to the cardboard (can be cut so that one side has a fold)

4 bolts about 4 inches (10 cm) long with wing nuts

Method

1 Drill holes in the corners of each piece of plywood so that the bolts will go through vertically. It is advisable to place the boards together and to drill through both at the same time.

2 Cut the corners off the cardboard and blotting paper sheets so that they will fit between the bolts.

3 Starting with cardboard, add two sheets of blotting paper and one of cardboard. Place these between the boards, insert the bolts and screw the wing nuts on the top of each bolt.

COLLECTING PLANT MATERIAL

Some patience is necessary when you decide to make a pressed flower picture because unfortunately you cannot decide to do it one night and make it the next day. You must have a stock of pressed plant material which takes several months to dry before you can use it. The best thing to do is to get started with the pressing and then forget the next stage for a while. However, once you have begun pressing, you will build up a ready supply and can make pictures at any time of the year. Most people tend to press more than they need, which is a good fault.

The aim of pressing is to remove the water content of a flower or leaf and, at the same time, to flatten the material without wrinkling it. It is better to cut plant material on a dry day because if it is wet it takes even longer to dry and press and could become mouldy.

Perfect specimens are preferable for a picture that will endure for years, so avoid cutting damaged plant material — it only uses up the limited space in a press. Look for beautiful flowers and leaves at exactly the stage of maturity that you wish to preserve.

The thickness of a leaf or flower is of great importance. The most successful plant material is thin and also of a uniform thinness; before cutting a flower I always feel it gently all over to see if it is of an even thickness. A flower with a raised hard centre but thin petals, for example certain daisies, is a problem because the press reaches the centre first and the petals wrinkle while the centre is becoming flattened. But you can still press flowers like these by detaching the petals and pressing them separately from the centres.

Plant material to avoid

Thick, fleshy leaves such as those of sedums have a high water content and take a long time to press; the results are not usually attractive. Plant material with rigid tissue, like a holly leaf, does not press well either. Flowers with many petals such as full-blown peonies and roses are quite useless unless the petals are pressed separately; a rose or peony form can be reassembled and an impression of the flower formed from only a few petals.

Protected flowers

Since 1975 it has been illegal for anyone without permission from the landowner or occupier to uproot *any* wild plant. There are 21 plants that have been given special protection and picking or removal of any part of these plants is an offence. The protected plants are: Alpine gentian, Alpine snow-thistle, Alpine woodsia, blue heath, Cheddar pink, diapensia, drooping saxifrage, ghost orchid, Killarney fern, lady's slipper, mezereon, military orchid, monkey orchid, oblong woodsia, red helleborine, Snowdon lily, spiked speedwell, spring gentian, Teesdale sandwort, tufted saxifrage, wild gladiolus.

Ideal plant material

There is a wealth of suitable plant material. I look for small flowers and leaves with thin tissue and rather a flat structure. Rock plants are a good source of supply and there are many small wild flowers not on the conservation lists. Gardens and the countryside are full of material suitable for pressing and it does not have to be long-lasting in water as for a flower arrangement; short-lived flowers can also be used.

Seaweed

Delicate fronds of seaweed can be used alone or with other plant material in pictures and were a favourite of Victorian flower arrangers. When taken out of water seaweed loses its fern-like appearance, but this can be retained by floating the seaweed in a sink of deep water; slide a sheet of blotting paper into the water and under the seaweed, then lift it carefully out of the water carrying the seaweed with it. Leave to dry thoroughly before covering with a second sheet of blotting paper and placing in a press.

Size

I prefer flowers of the size of buttercups, primroses, violets and pansies, and some even smaller. A picture frame does not provide a large area in which to work and there is no scope for a design of larger flowers. The most admired pictures usually contain many smaller specimens. You will also need leaves of varying sizes.

Shape

It is important to have a variety of shapes. Buds and half-open flowers, or petals that can be assembled into a bud shape, are essential. A good design cannot be made with round flowers alone. You will also need some stems, otherwise the flowers will appear to float in space, and although sometimes you may want this effect, at other times you will need stems to 'anchor' the flowers. Thin, wiry ones such as those of buttercups, clematis and grasses are useful. Tendrils from wild vetch, a passion flower or sweet pea make lovely twirls in a picture. Straight stems can be gently curved by Sellotaping a strip of paper across them on to the blotting paper before pressing.

There are some flowers with unsuitable bulky centres that do not press well, so use other flowers for centres and make an interesting 'new flower'. Press a sheet of astrantias or other attractive small flowers for this purpose.

Seedheads such as dandelion provide interesting contrasts in shape, and grasses are invaluable for height. Long thin leaves are useful for transition in a design and ferns give a shape with an intricate outline.

A list of flowers and leaves is no help if you do not know plant names but this does not matter; just cut anything small and thin that attracts you in shape and colour. For those

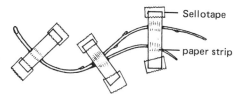

Sellotape

paper strip

Curving a stem before pressing

readers who know the names of the more familiar flowers and leaves, I find the following press well and are effective in designs:

Green
Grasses, geranium leaves (especially with markings), maidenhair fern, fern fronds, honeysuckle leaves, rose leaves, hellebore flowers, mosses, small leafed herbs, tobacco plant, auriculas, seaweed

Yellow and orange
Iceland poppies, marigold petals, celandines, buttercups, winter jasmine, laburnum, lady's mantle (*Alchemilla mollis*), autumn's yellowing leaves, primroses, polyanthus, pansies, primulas, broom, fennel flowers

Blue and mauve
Delphinium florets, lobelias pressed on their sides, campanulas cut in half, clematis, speedwell, periwinkle, rue foliage, forget-me-nots, larkspurs, hydrangea florets, pansies, violas, auriculas, gentians (split)

Red and pink
Geranium petals, astrantias, larkspurs, Virginia creeper foliage (small leaves), rose petals, tobacco plant flowers, primulas, polyanthus, seaweed, maple leaves, small poppies

White, cream beige, grey
Grasses, Queen Anne's lace, ox-eye daisies, field daisies, alyssum, hellebores, strawberry flowers, smaller narcissus, *Cineraria maritima* foliage, plume poppy (*Macleaya cordata*) (leaf back), blackberry foliage (leaf back)

COLOUR RETENTION

Pure colours retain their colouring better than subtle shades and tones:

blue can fade, though delphiniums and lobelias are reliable
brown retains colour
green stays green but fades
grey very successful retention
orange good colour retention
pink fairly good colour retention
purple turns brown or becomes very dark
red not good, usually turns brown, though some red geraniums
    retain colour
white can remain a good white or turn grey or cream depending
    on the flower
yellow excellent colour retention, especially bright yellow

PRESSING PLANT MATERIAL

Plant material should be pressed immediately after it has been cut, and the best thing to do is to take your press on a country visit. If you cannot do this, keep the material in a closed poly-thene bag until you reach home. There is no need to condition plant material beforehand; this only increases the water content. Wilted flowers should be discarded.

Flowers, leaves and stems are usually pressed separately, with a few exceptions such as half-open buttercups and other flowers with thin, wiry stems which can be pressed on the stem. Later the parts can be reassembled in the design. I find it easier to remove the bolts from the press before starting to add the plant material.

Cut off the stem close to the flower and place each flower carefully on a sheet of blotting paper. It is easier to place most flowers upside down and this makes no difference to the end result. There are few really flat flowers and most have a slight 'trumpet' shape; when placed face upwards they do not sit upright and a crease can result when pressed. Positioned upside down the flower is flattened more evenly. Flowers with more emphasised trumpets, such as harebells, can be halved length-ways. Cut them with small scissors and press as two flowers.

It is important for uniform pressure to place plant material of the same thickness on each sheet of blotting paper. It is also helpful to group the plant material into stems, flowers, buds or seedheads; you can then quickly find anything you need and without disturbing other material in the press.

Flowers and leaves can be placed close together, but if they overlap you risk being unable to separate them after pressing. When a sheet is full of plant material, carefully roll over a second sheet of blotting paper, then add a sheet of cardboard. Start again with another layer of blotting paper. Replace the top of the press when you have inserted all the plant material. Replace bolts, screw on the wing nuts and tighten. It is an essential part of pressing to tighten the nuts every day for about a week, or until they will tighten no more. This makes the plant material unwrinkled and paper thin. I find if I leave the press in the kitchen I am reminded to tighten the screws each day. After this the press can be stored anywhere, as long as it is in a dry atmosphere.

If you use heavy books or weights in place of a press, place the material between two sheets of blotting paper in the lower part of the book, but allow the paper to stick out so that you can see where the flowers are placed. If you write the contents and the date on the edge of the paper you will save time and disturbance. Five or six large, heavy books should be placed on top of the book containing the plant material.

Labelling

It really is sensible to label each sheet with the contents, such as 'stems', 'leaves', 'flowers', 'centres' and the date. Leave the label sticking out of the press so that it can be read easily. This saves disturbance and time in searching for a particular shape. The date will tell you how long each piece of plant material has

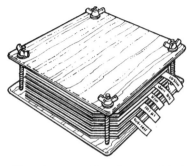

Closed press with reference labels
showing position of different
plant material

been in the press. If you do a lot of pressing you may want to divide into colours as well as shapes, or even into varieties if you press a lot of one type of flower or leaf.

Pressing time

The length of time necessary for adequate pressing is a matter of opinion. Some people say a month is long enough and others say colour retention is better when the plant material is left undisturbed for a year. This is a difficult matter on which to be definite because the results depend so much on the flower colour, the type of plant material and variations in the lighting of the setting in which a picture is hung. My own inclination is to leave plant material in the press as long as possible.

When new plant material is added place it in fresh sheets of blotting paper on top of those already in the press to save disturbing the material already in it.

STORING PRESSED MATERIAL

It is easier to store pressed material in the press than anywhere else. But if you need the space leave it within the blotting paper sheets and store in a box or inside a heavy book. Wherever the material is stored be sure that the atmosphere is dry because moisture can be re-absorbed.

RESTORING WRINKLED MATERIAL

You can sometimes press wrinkled plant material flat by using a warm iron or a steam iron. Place it between sheets of tissue paper and lower the iron gently on to it rather than ironing with a sideways movement. You have nothing to lose by trying this because you will probably not use the wrinkled material unless it can be flattened.

PRESSED FLOWER PICTURES

You will need
Picture frame with glass and a backing of hardboard or Dalorboard
Wire for hanging and two eye screws
Covering for the backing in the frame
Pressed plant material
Copydex or a latex-type adhesive which is removable without leaving a stain
Small, thin, flat knife
Small pointed scissors
Tweezers and a few cocktail sticks or toothpicks
Small paintbrush

The frame
A delicate frame is more suitable than a heavy frame because

pressed flowers have a dainty appearance. The shape and size is more important than the colour, which can be altered.

The shape is a matter of choice; it can be round, oval, square or rectangular. To a certain extent this decides the shape of your design because you will need to fill the framed background adequately. Glass can be ordinary or non-reflecting, which is slightly opaque and a little more expensive but with no shine at any angle.

You may be able to find old frames at low cost in markets and second-hand shops; alternatively, suitable frames can be bought in photographer's and art shops. Suppliers of flower arrangement material now carry good stocks. It is also possible to make a picture on a backing and then have it framed by a framer, but you risk disturbance to the plant material unless great care is taken.

It is important that the glass of the frame presses on to the design and is not raised above it. This helps to keep the plant material flat and in position.

The backing

The colour and texture of the background is an important part of the design. If most of the plant material is light, then a darker background will show it up well; darker plant material needs a lighter background. I group colours together, adding and subtracting until I am happy with the shapes and colours. I find it easier at this stage to group lighter and darker colours separately. This suggests the lightness or darkness of the background. Brilliant coloured backgrounds are never suitable because they detract from the delicate-coloured flowers which should be the important part of the picture. It is not advisable to use a similar shade to any seen in the plant material, which will be lost unless placed against plant material of another colour.

There are many materials that can be used for background mounting such as paper, fabric or cardboard. A rigid backing of hardboard under any of these is essential — the hardboard itself could be painted and used directly. There are beautiful papers available, sometimes hand-made from plants; these are expensive but you need only a little. You could also experiment with painting a subtle, shaded background straight on to the paper, thus combining the art of painting with that of making flower pictures. Fabrics could include thin jerseys, silks, cottons and felt, and they could be faded, tie-dyed or half-bleached to give unusual effects.

The background must be fully prepared before sticking on the plant material. Cover the hardboard backing of the frame with decorator's size using two coats and allowing it to dry in between. Press on the background, making sure there are no creases. It is helpful to have someone hold one end of the background when you place it down on the backing to ensure a flat surface. Turn over a half-inch (1cm) margin of fabric, which can fray easily, on to the reverse side, being very careful to keep the front perfectly clean. Glue down the edges on to the back, folding over the corners neatly. When paper, felt or non-fraying fabric is used, folding over is unnecessary, but the background should reach to the edges of the backing so that there is no gap. Wrap up the backing to keep it clean while you plan the design.

Method

I find it useful to cut a sheet of paper the same size as the background (light or dark according to the colour of the background) on which to design the image and then to transfer the design to the final background flower by flower.

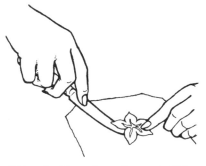

Slide a knife under a flower to lift

Lift the delicate pressed flowers with a knife, placing your finger gently on top to prevent them blowing away (they are very light). Tweezers can be used for some plant material such as stems, but can tear more delicate tissues. Move around the shapes and colours until you have a design that pleases you. If you must leave it at any stage roll over a sheet of blotting paper and add a weight, otherwise the design may be wafted apart by the slightest draught.

The next stage is to transfer the design to its permanent background. It is unnecessary to cover the complete back of a flower or leaf with adhesive. Use spots applied with a tooth-pick or cocktail stick; the less used the better because large amounts of adhesive sometimes seep through fine petals. Some people make a picture without any adhesive and rely on the glass to hold the plant material in position. But I feel happier with a little adhesive for safety. A paintbrush is useful for stroking petals into position and for turning flowers gently.

When all the plant material is glued into position, cover with the glass. It is important that the glass is perfectly clean on both sides before you do this. Try not to move the glass as this disturbs the plant material. Lift the glass and the backing, firmly held in both hands, and turn them over to lower into the upturned frame. Padding with paper or board may be necessary for a tight fit before you finally cover the back with masking tape, a sheet of brown paper or Fablon. Nailing the picture (as is done with canvas-backed paintings) is not advisable because it can disturb the design. Add eye screws for hanging up the picture and thread through a wire for hanging.

The design

There are many styles, naturalistic or stylised. You can make a circular bouquet or Victorian posy. You can arrange the flowers in a 'container' made of bark, fabric or other thin material so that they look like an arrangement of flowers. Garlands are attractive placed in a circle, square, oval or rectangle according to the shape of the frame. This style leaves the centre empty, but if you add stem twirls and smaller flowers towards the centre the emptiness is relieved. Plant material can also be

63 A pressed flower picture with overlapping petals to give a three-dimensional effect. (*Arranger* Mavis Brooker)

arranged as it grows, in groups springing from the 'ground' (which can be a line drawn on the background). Ideas can come from looking at paintings, friezes, advertisements, other flower arrangements and illustrations.

The usual basic principles of design apply: good balance, contrasts or variations in shape and visual texture, some areas of emphasis, good scaling and a pleasing proportion of plant material and background – neither over- or under-filled. The rhythm of the design depends on the style. You may decide on an upright design using many straight-stemmed flowers, or on curves. Repetition of shapes, colours and varieties of plant material is important and helps to achieve unity and rhytm.

In a two-dimensional design an impression of depth can only be achieved by overlapping flowers and leaves. Remember to glue on the pieces for the back of the design first. When using paper-thin plant material it can be overlapped so that other flowers or leaves show through, giving a delightfully ethereal effect.

Flowers of the same variety can be grouped and need not have added stems. The viewing eye can imagine the stems without your having to clutter the picture with them. But in other styles stems are necessary to give a more realistic appearance.

Composition

Most people enjoy combining many types of plant material together in order to have differing shapes and colours, but it can be fascinating to try other ideas of composition. You could use only one type of plant material in all stages of growth; for example, clematis flowers, stems, buds, leaves and seed-heads could make a 'botanical study' of the clematis. Grasses of many kinds would make a picture of great interest and so would leaves. Grey- and silver-leaved plants or the foliage of one family of plants such as eucalyptus could be fascinating, or you could use the autumn-coloured leaves of the maples. Herbs would make a good collection and be useful for identification purposes.

Pictures could be made depicting each season or different landscapes, such as seashore, meadow, mountain, woodland and lakeland. The moods of nature could be interpreted with a windswept style, a sunny day, misty weather, storm and so on. Or the rhythm of growth of one plant — erect, trailing, curving, climbing or bushy — could be emphasised.

HOLIDAY PICTURES

One of the most delightful ways of recording memories of a holiday is by making a picture using the plant material you have collected there. Take a small press with you so that the flowers and leaves can be pressed at once.

It is helpful to make notes about the atmosphere, local colourings and geographical features so that you have a record of your immediate impressions. This reminds you of your holiday and helps to inspire the picture, which will be made some time after your return.

Subtle colours of purples, blues and greys with rough textures could evoke memories of Scotland. A blue background with white flowers and exotic leaves could remind you of Bermuda, while ferns, bark, small daffodils and primroses could be reminiscent of a country holiday.

GREETING CARDS

You can make your own mounting cards or buy ready-made cards especially made for pressed flowers. Once you have had some practice in making greeting cards many variations will probably occur to you such as adding coloured borders in contrasting colours, glueing on calendars, spray-painting round the

64 A landscape design using pressed plant material. (*Arranger* Margaret Cash)

design (which should be protected with cut-to-shape card), inking in thin or thick ruled lines around the edge, or using felt-tipped pens for border lines. When selecting plant material for a card, scale is a special consideration and the design should be in proportion to the card.

Home-made cards

Arrange the pressed flower design on a cut-out circle, oval, rectangle or square sheet of thin white or coloured card and glue down as you would do for a pressed flower picture (page 131). Cover with a sheet of matt, transparent self-adhesive film, obtainable from a stationer, to protect the plant material. Cut the film to the shape of the background after pressing it on. Another pair of hands can be useful when handling the film so that it can be stretched to avoid creases. The protected design is now ready to glue on to a folded sheet of paper or card in a second colour.

Ready-made cards

There are a number of variations in card material including matt finish cards with embossed borders and deckle edges in a number of shapes and sizes; notelet blanks, dinner place cards, book-mark blanks, botanical specimen cards and gift tags. There are also two-fold cards with a centre window frame. The design is made on one side, covered with film and folded into the frame, making a normal one-fold card.

A three-fold card with: (a) window frame; (b) self-adhesive backing; (c) back fold bearing a printed greeting

TABLE MATS

You first need to find a professional, or keen amateur photographer who has a heat-sealing machine. This applies an unbreakable and stain-resistant light film to surfaces and protects them. It is available in a number of surface textures such as plain or linen finish. It is normally used for bonding to the surfaces of photographs and maps.

1 Perforate the film with a multi-wheel piercing tool to prevent the retention of moisture under the film once it has been bonded.

2 Arrange pressed flowers on Formica cut to your chosen shape and size.

3 Place the film over the design, being especially careful not to disturb the flowers. This may take time. Trim off surplus film.

4 A special foam plastic sheet and a thin sheet of metal, to disperse the heat evenly, are then placed by the photographer over the film and all placed into the ready-heated press for about 20 minutes.

5 The mats can be backed with hardboard and green baise or felt to make a soft surface on a polished wood dining table.

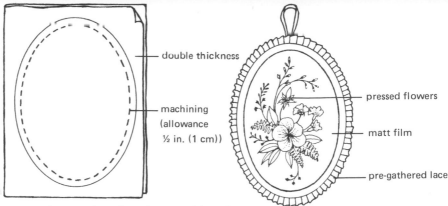

Pressed flower decoration for the outside of a pot-pourri sachet

double thickness

machining (allowance ½ in. (1 cm))

pressed flowers

matt film

pre-gathered lace

POT-POURRI SACHETS

Pressed flowers make a pretty decoration for the outside of a sachet of pot-pourri. These make useful small gifts and sell well at bazaars.

1 Use a template or any round or oval object of the required size and pencil round on thin fabric.

2 Machine on the line through a double thickness of fabric (on the wrong side) and leave a space at the top for tuning inside out.

3 Cut out leaving a half-inch (1cm) seam allowance.

4 Turn the 'envelope' inside out and press flat.

5 Glue a design of pressed flowers on one side.

6 Cover with self-adhesive matt film and cut this to fit the sachet. This is important for protection of the flowers.

7 Fill the sachet with pot-pourri, insert a ribbon loop for hanging if you wish and sew up the gap.

8 Glue or sew on an edging of pre-gathered lace.

DOOR FINGERPLATES

Transparent Perspex plates to protect doors from finger marks can be bought and can look very attractive when decorated with pressed flowers.

1 Cut a piece of cardboard to fit into the back of the plate.

2 Cover the card with thin fabric, Sellotaping the raw edges to the back of the card.

3 Glue on the flowers and then place the card into the doorplate so that the design shows but is protected by Perspex.

PAINTING PRESSED PLANT MATERIAL

Fading does occur with pressed flowers subjected constantly to daylight, such as in a picture hanging on a wall. Soft colours can be applied with waterbased paint after pressing. If this does not adhere to the petal surface easily, add a small drop of washing-up liquid to the paint. Often stroking on touches of very pale tints is sufficient and the flowers need not be completely covered with paint. But remember that as the natural colour fades the paint will appear garish unless a soft colour is chosen to start with.

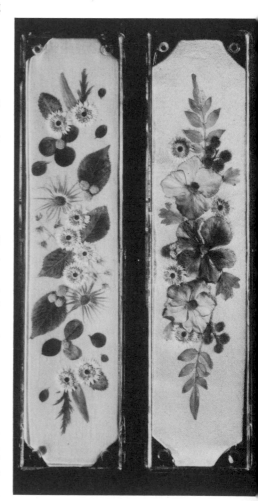

65 Door fingerplates decorated with pressed flowers. (*Arranger* Catherine Parry)

10 PLANTS GROWN IN GLASS CONTAINERS

Plants grown in glass enclosures need little attention for weeks, even months on end. This makes them ideal for people who like something living and green in their homes but are often away or have little time for watering. They are also useful decoration for a weekend cottage because they can be left unattended for so long. They are often called bottle gardens although many other shapes of glass container can be used. 'Terrarium' is another word used for any transparent container with a sealed covering or a small opening.

An 'other world' effect can be obtained, which is quite fascinating, especially in a large container with a variety of small plants. The principle is that when sealed, the bottle or container keeps all moisture inside. The plants transpire through their leaves, but the moisture does not escape. It condenses on the inside of the glass and returns to the soil to be taken up once more by the roots. The atmosphere is balanced and the plants take up oxygen at night and give off carbon dioxide in daylight.

CONTAINERS

In Victorian times elegant Wardian cases were used. The name came from Dr Nathaniel Ward who about 150 years ago discovered that plants, especially tropical plants, could flourish unattended in a closed glass container. You can sometimes find modern versions of these cases but they are expensive.

However, there are many inexpensive glass and plastic containers that can be used. The glass must be clear to let in the light but it does not matter if it is green or white. Acid carboys are ideal because they are large, but they have become hard to obtain because they are no longer made in England and have to be imported. There are also wine and cider flagons, large preserving jars, sweet and storage jars with glass stoppers, fish bowls, aquarium tanks with a sheet of glass for a lid, old battery jars, ball jars and a variety of clear plastic containers (these must be made of rigid, thick plastic such as Perspex).

Containers such as aquarium tanks are easy to plant because you can put your hands inside them easily. A container with a narrow neck is more difficult and requires patience and special tools (see below), although once planted it needs little attention. It does look more mysterious, rather like the mystery of a ship in a bottle, and your friends will wonder how you managed to plant it. Simple purpose-built terrariums have a fitted lid and adjustable air vents. There are also more elaborate designs, like a miniature conservatory, with heating equipment and artificial lighting.

You can also make a terrarium by placing a glass dome over a container of plants, making sure it fits tightly inside the rim of the container. It is advisable to buy the dome first because they can be difficult to find, and then buy a container to fit it.

TOOLS

No tools are necessary for containers with openings large enough for your hands to go through, but for containers with small openings it is necessary to have long-handled small tools for planting and occasional attention. You can buy these tools at garden centres; alternatively, you can make your own. A table fork tied securely to a long stick or cane makes a good rake. A teaspoon on a stick can act as a spade and a cotton-reel glued to a dowel stick is excellent for tamping down the soil around plants. A razor blade wedged into a slit in a stick can be used for pruning, and a long steel knitting needle is use-

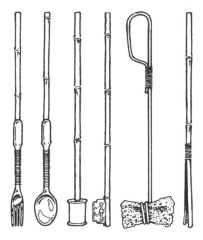

Simple home-made tools for planting up a glass container

66 An attractive mixture of various plants. **Top**: *Dracaena sanderiana, Codiaeum variegatum pictum* (Croton) **Centre**: *Hedera Helix 'Glacier', Saintpaulia, Peperomia magnoliaefolia 'Variegata'* **Bottom**: *Asplanium nidus, Crypthanthus acaulis 'Rubra', Cryptanthus bivitattus, Hedera Helix 'Discolour'*

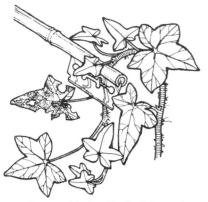

A razor blade attached to a piece of bamboo can be used to cut away dead growth which might cause mildew

You can clean the inside of the bottle using a damp sponge held in an improvised wire loop

ful for piercing and removing fallen leaves. A pair of sticks used like chopsticks can also do this job. A sponge tied to a stick or in a strong wire loop is useful for wiping the inside of the bottle. If you can find long-handled tongs, or adapt kitchen tongs by lengthening the handles, these are most useful for handling plants.

PLANTING UP THE CONTAINER

This is the only part of creating a bottle garden that needs patience, but once planted you can almost forget about it.

You will need
Freshly washed container that is quite clean
Small plants, seedlings and rooted cuttings which like similar conditions
Drainage material such as gravel or pebbles
Charcoal
Packet of John Innes No. 2 potting compost, or sand if you choose to plant cacti.
It is important to buy the soil from a garden centre because it will be sterilised and free of bugs and bacteria which would be difficult to eradicate in a bottle garden.

Method
1 Mix some charcoal with the drainage material to keep the water sweet.
2 Using a cardboard tube with a narrow-necked container add a 1 inch (2.5cm) layer of the drainage material for a small container, 2 inches (5cm) for a larger container.
3 Damp but do not soak the potting compost and add it using a cardboard tube and/or a paper funnel to keep the sides of the bottle clean, until you have twice the depth of the drainage material (5 inches (12cm) is enough for a large carboy). The compost can be built up into 'hills and valleys' if you wish. Push the soil down using a cotton-reel tamper.
4 If the compost was rather dry, add water, running it down the sides of the bottle, but avoid soggy compost.
5 Make a depression with the 'spade' where you wish each plant to go; start planting from the outside working inwards.
6 Push the 'rake' into the root ball of each plant, tilting the bottle slightly if necessary. Wriggle free the rake and then use the tamper to push down the soil around the plant. (Alternatively use bamboo 'tweezers' to insert small plants.) To avoid soiling the sides of the bottle wrap each plant in a paper cone to lower it into the compost and then pull out the paper.
7 Keep the roots away from the sides of the container so that the leaves, as they grow, will not be squashed against the sides of the glass; it is also advisable to allow space around each plant so that it can grow on and not crowd its neighbours.

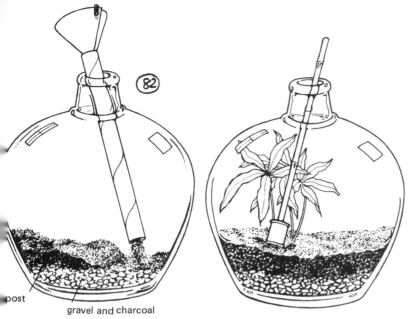

post
gravel and charcoal

DESIGN

Careful thought should be given in the design of the garden. Taller growing plants can be used at the back and spreading ones in the front. There also needs to be some contrast in leaf pattern, shape and colour, as well as habit of growth, to add interest in your garden.

AFTERCARE

The correct level of humidity is reached when there is a slight film of moisture on the inside of a closed container. However, containers that are completely sealed can become steamed up so that you cannot see the plants. In this case there must be some ventilation and the lid should be removed or slightly opened. This may mean an occasional watering to make up for what is lost through the opening.

A closed-up bottle can go for a year or more without watering if you have the correct level of humidity, but watch for dryness if you have an open top or a ventilation gap.

Keep the bottle garden or terrarium out of direct summer sun but in good light. Turn it occasionally so that light falls evenly on the plants.

SUITABLE PLANTS

Foliage plants are the most suitable for planting in a glass container. African violets enjoy the conditions of a bottle garden, but other flowering plants fade quickly and then you have the job of removing dead flowers. Slow-growing small plants are the most suitable.

Flexible leaves are easier to plant in a narrow-necked container and plants in 3inch (7cm) diameter pots are suitable in size. About six can be planted in a standard carboy.

Far left Using a funnel and cardboard tube, pour in a layer of gravel and crushed charcoal, followed by the soil mixture
Left Tamp down the soil around the plants with a cotton-reel wedged firmly to the end of a piece of bamboo cane or dowel stick
Above Use bamboo 'tweezers' to insert smaller plants and to move plants into their final position

Protect larger plants with a cylinder of rolled paper before lowering them into place

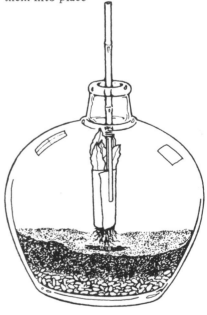

67 *Opposite* An interesting grouping of plants is always something to consider. Here the placement of the bottle garden in the window leading to a conservatory filled with plants adds an extra dimension to the colourful scene

Plant	Description	Comments
Acornus gramineus	Grass-like	
Adiantum	Maidenhair fern, light green triangular fronds on black stalks	
Cocos (syagus) weddeliana	Dwarf coconut palm	use only small plant
Cryptanthus	variously coloured rosettes	
Cryptobergia rubra	Bromelaid	
Episcia cupreata	red undersides to leaves	
Ficus pumila	creeping fig, climber or trailer with small green ovate leaves	prune regularly
Fittonia	Creeping plants with colourful veined leaves	
Hedera	Ivy, green and variegated	small leaved forms only suitable
Maranta	Ovate leaves, green with brown-purple blotches between lateral veins	
Neanthe bella	Dwarf palm	use only small plant
Pellionia pulchra	Creeping herbs with coloured stems	prune regularly
Peperomia caperata	Leaves dark green with purple corrugations, flower spikes like mice tails	
Pilea	Oblong ovate leaves, dark green with silvery patches between veins	prune regularly
Pteris	Ferns with ribbon-like fronds	
Saintpaulia	African violet, one of the few flowering plants recommended. Variety of colour from deep purple to pale pink (single & double)	flowers must be removed immediately they die back
Saxifraga stolonifera tricolour	Mother of thousands. This variety is a slower grower than others of the same species	
Sellaginella apus	Moss-like plants allied to ferns. Fronds creeping or erect, branched, green or variegated	

List of suppliers

Paperweight casting kits
Strand Glassfibre Ltd, Brentway Trading Estate, Brentford, Middlesex.

Seed merchants
Thomas Butcher, 60 Wickhams Road, Shirley, Croydon, Surrey.
Samuel Dobie & Sons Ltd, Upper Dee Mills, Llangollen, Clwyd.
Hurst Garden Pride, Hyde Industrial Estate, The Hyde, London NW9.
Suttons Seeds, Hele Road, Torquay, Devon.
Thompson & Morgan Ltd, London Road, Ipswich, Suffolk.
W.J. Unwin Ltd, Histon, Cambridge.

Greetings cards for pressed flowers
Impress, Slough Farm, Westhall, Halesworth, Suffolk, IP19 8RN.
Prestacard Picture Mounts, 42 Brighton Road, Surbiton, Surrey KT6 5PL.

Recommended reading

Bulbs
Mathew, B., *Dwarf Bulbs,* Batsford 1973
Mathew, B., *Larger Bulbs,* Batsford 1978
Synge, P. M., *Guide to Bulbs,* Collins 1961
Witham Fogg, H.G., *The Complete Handbook of Bulbs,* Ward Lock 1973

Dried and preserved flower decorations
Condon, G, *Complete Book of Flower Preservation,* Robert Hale 1974
Derbyshire, J. & Burgess R, *Dried and Pressed Flowers,* Hamlyn 1975
Foster, M., *Creating Pictures with Preserved Flowers,* Pelham Books 1977
McDowall, P., *Pressed Flower Collages and Other Ideas,* Lutterworth
  Press 1975
McDowall, P., *Pressed Flower Pictures,* Lutterworth Press 1975
McWilliam, & Shipman, D., *Everlasting Flower Craft Step by Step,* David
  & Charles 1975
Morrison, W., *Drying and Preserving Flowers,* Batsford 1973
Nichol, K, *Flowers For Pleasure,* Lutterworth Press 1975

Foliages to grow
Emberton, S., *Garden Foliage for Flower Arrangement,* Faber 1968
Emberton, S., *Shrub Gardening for Flower Arrangement,* Faber 1973
MacQueen, S., *Flower Arranging from Your Garden,* Ward Lock 1977
Nehrling, A. & I., *Gardening for Flower Arrangement,* Dover Press 1976
Smith, G., *Flower Arranging in House and Garden,* Pelham Books 1977
Witham Fogg, H.G., *The Fower Arranger's Garden,* Pelham Books 1978

General flower arranging
Taylor, J., *Creative Flower Arrangement,* Stanley Paul 1973
Taylor, J., *Flower Arranging,* Macdonald 1978
Taylor, J., *Practical Flower Arranging,* Hamlyn 1974
Vagg, D., *Flower Arranging,* Ward Lock 1980
Webb, I., *Complete Guide to Flower and Foliage Arrangements,* Webb
  & Bower 1979

Houseplants
Rochford, T., & Gorer, R., *Book of House Plants,* Faber 1973
Wright, M., *(ed.) The Complete Indoor Gardener,* Pan 1974

Modern flower arrangement
Aaronson, M., *Design with Plant Material,* Grower Books 1972
Brack, E., *Flower Arrangement: Free Style,* Whitethorn Press 1977
Reister, D., *Design for Flower Arrangers,* Van Nostrand Reinhold 1964

Periodicals
Flora — published bi-monthly by Stanley Gibbons Magazines, Drury
  House, Russell Street, London WC2B 5HD
The Flower Arranger — published quarterly by NAFAS. Obtainable
  through flower clubs or by direct subscription from Taylor-Bloxham,
  Tyrell Street, Leicester LE3 5SB
The Florist Trade Magazine — published monthly by Lonsdale Publications
  Ltd, 120 Lower Ham Road, Kingston-upon-Thames, Surrey

Index